FRONTIERS OF CHANGE

Frontiers of Change:

Early Industrialism in America

Thomas C. Cochran

New York   Oxford
OXFORD UNIVERSITY PRESS
1981

Library of Congress Cataloging in Publication Data

Cochran, Thomas Childs, 1902–
    Frontiers of change.

    Bibliography: p.
    Includes index.
    1. United States—Economic conditions—To 1865.
    2. United States—Industries—History.
    3. United States—Social conditions—To 1865.
    4. Technological innovations—United States—
    History.   I. Title.
    HC105.C64   338.0973   80-20788
    ISBN 0-19-502875-9

Printed in the United States of America

Acknowledgments

In preparing this book I have had the advantage of a number of years as Senior Resident Scholar at the Eleutherian Mills–Hagley Foundation and as chairman of the advisory committee for its Regional Economic History Research Center. I am indebted for bits and pieces of my analysis to all the scholars who have frequented the library during the last half dozen years and to the writers of papers for its regional meetings. I particularly want to thank Eugene S. Ferguson, Tony A. Freyer, Brooke Hindle, Diane Lindstrom, William Mulligan, Jr., Glenn Porter, Julian Skaggs, Merritt Roe Smith, and Anthony F. C. Wallace for good advice and reading parts of the manuscript. Without the aid of Carolyn Johnson and Debra Bowers it would never have been put together. At Oxford University Press, Nancy Lane gave the book special attention, and Ann Hofstra Grogg was a truly creative copy editor.

Thomas C. Cochran

Radnor Pa.
September 1980

Contents

FRONTIERS OF CHANGE

Introduction

This essay is intended to be far broader in its implications than the subtitle suggests. The coming of industrialism to America is selected as an example of how societies in general evolve new structures, new beliefs, and new patterns of action. Whether innovations come in technology, religion, or politics, they are the result of people's experience with life, their accumulated knowledge, and their aspirations, or with what anthropologists call "culture." Culture has, necessarily, to be in tune with geography, although there are certain dissonances as technology or movements of population alter basic geo-cultural relationships. The view presented here may be called geo-cultural.

All of history is the more or less imperfect record of geo-cultural relationships. Social scientists, particularly economists, are trained to formulate discrete categories and models involving actions that follow defined and, it is to be hoped, measurable forces. Delving as deeply as sources permit into past culture and finding little that is discrete or measurable, the scholar has to depend on "historical vision." [1] Earlier cultures have to be reconstructed from manifestations in events and writings, and certain of their aspects can never be known precisely but must be arrived at imaginatively. The level and type of knowledge a culture achieves is not a static accumulation fully ascertainable from its books and letters. It also involves the subtleties of how or why facts are known and of those intuitive urges that may lead to esthetic or artistic creative action. These must be reconstructed from looking at a culture's innovations, which may go beyond the level and type of knowledge suggested by its major events and recorded in its writings. A thoughtful economic scholar of innovation has written, "Presumably what we invent is the joint product of what we want and what we know."[2] Yet American mechanics in the early years of the Republic, and undoubtedly some of those in other nations at other times, innovated by inspirations that do not seem to stem immediately from the culture's generalized wants or from its general knowledge. Leonardo da Vinci had, of course, a background in Western culture, but his drawings, too, involved an esthetic creation that we cannot explain merely by rationally reconstructing the knowable, measurable factors of his situation.

The possibilities open to a people of any culture are either limited or augmented by geography and natural resources. Since each national and even regional culture is different from all others, the kind of esthetic or creative responses that each achieves will be unique. This essay attempts to trace the particular types of creative response to opportunities for material change that arose in post-Revolutionary America and to draw some contrasts with the responses in Britain to somewhat, but not exactly, similar situations.

Increases in production that stem from culture-bound phenomena can be measured, but the underlying cultural forces cannot. In the case of America, and many other nations, the absence of reliable statistics makes the whole study of early industrialization one of evaluating events and trends largely from qualitative and incomplete records. Hence the cultural approach has to carry the analysis. But outside of a general lack of reliable statistics—not very important in any case for this type of study—the record from 1775 to 1850 is quite voluminous. In addition to a considerable number of company and personal manuscripts, there is a large body of secondary literature that has never been properly synthesized from the standpoint of the essentials of industrial development. Most of the important secondary material, and many of the original records, are in the Eleutherian Mills Historical Library, Greenville, Delaware. In addition, in the 1950s the Hagley Museum commissioned numerous special reports on early industry and workers, particularly in the Brandywine Valley. Footnotes citing these and other studies are used chiefly to indicate further sources of information. Figures from the decadal censuses are not documented. Readers interested in pursuing a geo-cultural approach into later history may see my *Business in American Life*.

1
Why America and Britain?

The rulers of Saudi Arabia and numerous other men currently responsible for the development of nations must crave to know the critical factors in the rapid British and American industrialization of the late eighteenth century. Can history tell them the absolute essentials, or were there any? So far, scholarly study has failed to provide simple answers, and argument is as lively in the 1980s as it was a century ago. Economists place varying weight on such factors as a demand that could be readily increased by lowering prices, new technology producing cheaper supplies, better mobilization of capital through financial institutions, and changes in economic organization and business attitudes.[1] But why, at that particular time, did social forces, relatively stable and well adjusted to each other for hundreds of years, move in new directions that disrupted the traditional order? History has offered broad answers, such as a previous "commercial revolution" that had opened up worldwide trade, or the pursuit of the national aspirations of aggressive monarchies, or the rise of scientific thought and experimentation. But all of these must seem too general or remote to satisfy either historians wanting to know more exactly how change occurred or current planners having to allot specific resources.

I

In addition, no one of these primary causes nor all of them together explain the fact that among the many countries of the North Atlantic and Mediterranean communities the industrial revolution occurred most rapidly in two English-speaking nations. At the beginning of the eighteenth century Britain had no marked superiority over France, Switzerland, the Low Countries, the Hanseatic cities, or the Mediterranean region in basic or accessible knowledge of commercial or technological matters. Americans, who had only recently knit together commercially remote ports on the fringes of the continental wilderness, seemed even less likely to be leaders. Yet in the ensuing century and a half Britain and the United States became rapidly growing industrial nations while the others were hardly getting a start.

Historians have given a number of reasons for this remarkable lead, although most of these writers have not been sufficiently familiar with the advance of American technological development. One line of reasoning is that the feudal system and its comprehensive net of cultural values had a stronger hold on continental Europe than on the English-speaking world. Another calls attention to geographical conditions more favorable to transportation in Britain and the northeastern United States. Obviously these two nations were not troubled as much as continental Europe by the devastation of wars. Or the most simple answer of all sees the continuance of an initial eighteenth-century speedup as the result of natural resources: of abundant wood for the charcoal smelting of widespread iron ore in America or of good coking coal near to such ore in Britain. This last argument has been elaborated to show that British coal metallurgy early gained a lead that France could not overcome.[2] All of these answers contain partial truths and can be fitted into a more generalized model of favorable conditions. But in themselves they produce no agreement on first causes or prime movers; from them it is impossible to make even a tentative list of "necessities" for the continued change from a relatively static, traditional society to a dynamic society built on innovations in agriculture, commerce, and industry.

Furthermore, the muse of history seems to have playfully scattered false clues about what happened in Great Britain. On the surface it appears that mechanization of textile manufacture was the leading edge of a general industrialization. But subsequent history belies any generalization, for in the following two centuries many agricultural nations mechanized textile manufacture and then went no farther toward an industrial revolution. Obviously the jennies in spinning mills in eighteenth-century America and Britain were not basic causes, but only manifestations of deeper social forces. Similarly, the example of Britain suggests that steampower is a prerequisite for industrialization, yet textile and other mills on the Northeast Coast of America were usually located out in the countryside, along rivers, to take advantage of much-cheaper waterpower.

II

In recent years scholars on both sides of the Atlantic have seen the false character of some of the old material clues and have moved in the general direction of cultural explanations for industrialization. The meaning of culture has not changed in essence since its initial formulation by Edward B. Tylor over a century ago, but the implications of his definition of a "complex whole which includes knowledge, belief, art, morals, law, custom and any other capabilities and habits acquired by man as a member of society" have been elaborated on as applied to social problems. From the standpoint of the present study, Anthony F. C. Wallace's formulation is useful. He sees culture, in part, as "those ways of behavior or techniques of solving problems which, being more frequently and more closely approximated than other ways, can be said to have a high probability of use by individual members of society." Ward B. Goodenough illustrates another facet of the same general point of view by defining culture as the concepts and models that people have in their minds for organizing and interpreting their experience.[3] By applying these formulations to the American colonies and states, one might observe that the Northeast Coast had a majority or modal culture, based on its traditions and environment, that recognized innovations in craftsmanship and business policy as essential "techniques of solving problems." In addition, the necessities of the developing colonies and states enforced a continued emphasis on utilitarian ways of "organizing and interpreting . . . experience," one generation after another.

While Wallace and others see culture as capable of change, they recognize the strength of traditional elements and hence the origins of some American traits in the European background. Both economists such as John U. Nef and noneconomic social scientists recognize that cultural commitment to material improvement arose in Europe, at least, as early as the period of colonization.[4] Max Weber argued that a suitable religion was important. As the American experience shows, applying the artisan knowledge of mature European culture to overcoming the problems of a wilderness was highly educational; and as Britain demonstrated, the favorable social influences of skilled artisans, commercial entrepreneurs, interested aristocrats, and tolerably friendly government were important stimulants. But the generally propitious culture must also have had some special characteristics if the great advances around 1800 are to be explained.

In America and Britain of the eighteenth century there were already widespread wood and metal working industries, which, in these cultures at least, seem to have been crucial. The technological innovations that started the upsurge of industrialization, that is, were congenial to the existing culture and not, as in the case of less-developed nations, exotic imports. While the later Japanese experience might argue that "high technology" industries can be introduced by experienced artisans who have studied foreign machinery, this observation merely adds the corollary that, even if rapidly enlarged, a traditional, indigenous metalworking industry, like Japan's, was essential to bringing in the age of iron and steel.[5] Since later industrial machines continued to be made of metal, history assures us by hindsight that the metalworking industry was the essential of advanced technology in 1800. The particular needs of future development in an age of chemistry and electronics may not be so clear. Furthermore, the early industrial nations progressed chiefly in response to consumer demands, not by government acquisition of exotic equipment belonging to more developed societies.

In any period, a favorable general culture that has produced the right type of indigenously advancing technology seems essential in the environment upon which new economic conditions of supply, demand, and capital come to operate. Anglo-American culture in general serves to explain eighteenth-century inventors such as James Watt or Oliver Evans, while the governmental institutions common to the two nations helped by giving entrepreneurs legal security and freedom to act. Also, by providing relatively high protection against the ravages of war, politics, or other nonmarket forces, both governments encouraged rapid private investment.

There is nothing novel, per se, in listing as essentials to rapid development a favorable culture, a well-developed artisan background in the proper industries, freedom for entrepreneurial action, and a high degree of governmental security against interference, although continuous wars on the European continent after 1793 gave unusual importance to this last factor. The view put forward here, however, is that the long-run force of these factors is not dependent on market conditions at any given time. The long-run forces are qualitative aspects of the society and its culture, and, for meanings useful for other periods, history should be pursued on this institutional level. Innovators had to succeed in the market, but their successes are a measure of results rather than causes. The statistics, unreliable as they are, can only suggest what happened, not why it happened. As the philosopher William Barrett has cautioned, "Thinking must learn again to descend into the poverty of its materials."[6]

III

In tracing the social patterns that led to rapid industrial growth, it is necessary to examine particular cultural characteristics in more detail and, because this is a study of America, how these operated in its particular culture. At the very core of cultural difference between America and other nations, including Britain, was a greater interest by the urban upper class and most of the well educated in improving material devices. For example, the American Philosophical Society in Philadelphia, the largest city, honored men who worked on practical problems, while the great hereditary landed aristocrat Robert Livingston of New York financed experimental steamboats.

This basic regard for the practical or useful is reflected in many characteristics of American culture, including, among others, the relationship of the business community to the law courts and to new legislation. Under the pressure of lawyers the courts became distinctly favorable to entrepreneurial action.[7] Starting initially from the colonists' desire to buy and sell land freely, the common law in America grew to favor the operator, or internal developer, sometimes at the expense of absentee investors or the traditional rights of land owners. European, including English, land law had grown up around the concept of security both for inheritance and against harmful changes in the environment. American land law grew around facility of improvement and transfer. But the effects stretched far beyond the land; business transactions were freed from a mass of archaic legal ceremony. Guilds, for example, were never powerful in America, and cities readily granted artisan's licenses, where necessary, to all applicants. Associations of master craftsmen were never able to exercise exclusive controls over journeymen. After 1750 business lawyers came to be the shapers of new judicial interpretations. Ease of incorporation and protection of contracts against state interference were post-Revolutionary stimulants to investment. While successful industrialization without leadership from the business community and its lawyers seems almost unthinkable, the importance of their contribution has been too often overlooked.

Since it is men from the existing mercantile system who commission or invest in internal improvements, a well-coordinated and flexible business system seems a basic cultural prerequisite for rapid economic development. In America up to 1820, at least, efficient communication, transportation, finance, marketing, and law, all products of the business system, were collectively more important in reducing costs than were contemporary improvements in the fabrication of goods. It pleased early nineteenth-century Americans to have the price of cottons reduced, but the "new world" they lived in was more the product of faster and cheaper finance, trade, and transportation than the result of steam engines, power saws, and other new machines. Speeding the movement of goods from maker to receiver was the chief economizer of scarce working capital.

Inseparably associated with the dynamic American business system of the late eighteenth century were exceptionally flexible workbench artisans—men who knew how to use tools and could improve on old processes. Outside of American or British cultures, the relative lack of such all-purpose artisans was a major block to development. The United States in particular benefited from the generalized abilities of this group. In Europe artisans tended to become highly skilled at a particular craft, whereas in America migration and the ever-present need for new construction tended to make the artisan omnicompetent, on at least a moderate level. Consequently, many artisans moved readily from making furniture or hoes to erecting textile machinery and ultimately to fashioning parts for steam engines; or from building houses to constructing paper mills; or from working for wages to becoming independent entrepreneurs. Americans were short on book learning or artistic craftsmanship but long on know-how for building crude but effective machines. These traits were the result of the total culture acting on its members over generations. They were probably transmitted from generation to generation more by observation and practice than by formal apprenticeship or schooling, making for a flexible labor supply of relatively high competence.

After 1790 the interdependence of business and technical skills rapidly increased where concentrations of population made for easy communication. Regions favored by this concentration can industrialize independently of the nation as a whole. In a large urban area the man who wants credit can apply to a nearby bank; the shop superivsor who needs a new part can walk a few blocks down the street to get it. The innovator with a fresh inspiration can study existing practices, talk with informed friends, and consult useful books at hand. Historians of technology have come to think that it is from this working with new machines in locally competitive production—from this stage of trial and error in and around urban centers—that the large gains in efficiency arose. Seen another way, a concentration of workshops produces an informal all-purpose machine tool industry, and such an industry seems essential to autonomous growth or successful borrowing. The inescapable element in progressive industrialization appears to be machines for making machines. Furthermore, history indicates that once this stage of development has been reached, regression will come only from powerful external factors such as exhaustion of resources, war, or other major social disturbances.

IV

A conscious decision to innovate is governed by an artisan's or businessman's perception of the possibilities open to him. Philosophers and social scientists alike agree that what is perceived depends on what is already known; one sees what is behind the eyes rather than in front of them. Therefore, perception that leads to development is a matter of culture. The vision of the innovator is guided by generally held knowledge and social conditioning; the businessman manipulating the elements of his trade may instinctively see the possibility of new uses or combinations because the culture has encouraged artistic creativity. The tendency to innovation and ready acceptance of the new in American culture had unique qualities stemming from the total historic environment.

To begin with, the colonists came from the European frontiers of change in respect to business and technology. By their decision to migrate, to risk the formidable dangers of a trans-Atlantic voyage from which perhaps a quarter to a third would die, they must have represented a segment of European populations with an unusual willingness to take new risks.[8] Upon arriving, many went to partially settled areas where learning different ways of doing things was necessary to survival. The ways of life arising from continual migration into new areas, which at one time or another affected a large percentage of eighteenth-century Americans, also led to new ways of doing business and making things.

One writer has gone so far as to say Americans developed a "habit of habit change."[9]

As in the rest of the Western world, public education was minimal and apprenticeship was relied on for training in crafts, including housework and cooking, but in America no social stigma was attached to the status of apprentice. Wealthy planters apprenticed their sons to merchants, and the latter often preferred to have their sons trained by experience in another office. It was this type of education that was by 1780 partly responsible for a group of American businessmen and artisans who appear to have been as able as any in the world.

Continual migration produced a large group of consumers who were satisfied with crude articles. The migrant to a new settlement made what was needed. He often shifted readily from one occupation to another. Americans, in general, became jacks-of-all-trades, and perhaps true masters of none. The results of this experience were to show in the adoption of machinery. American craftsmen had great confidence that they could make machinery work. Often they failed to do so profitably, but occasionally in trying they made important innovations, like those of John Fitch and James Rumsey in steamboats, for example.

In addition, continual migration accentuated the open class structure of society. The new arrival in a community was judged by what he could do rather than who his parents were. There were, of course, exceptions at both top and bottom of this largely horizontal society. At the top were large merchants and landowners who in the Northeast were usually also investors in a number of commercial activities. At the bottom were men lacking in either ability or character, who worked as laborers, and also able young men who started in this status but soon became landowners, skilled artisans, or traders. None of these generalizations apply to enslaved black men who were not numerous in the areas of early industrialization. But the potential for upward mobility no doubt inspired most young men in America in a way not possible in more stratified societies.

High mobility, both geographic and social, also weakened family ties; men expected to leave home early, and in many cases the farm of their childhood memories was soon sold. The same was true of family business firms. Few sons felt the obligation, common in continental Europe, to perpetuate the farm or firm as a family enterprise. Money, or "economic rationality," rather than land or family ties, was the common measuring rod of the society. New opportunities drew away the ablest young men, and partnerships continually changed. Seen from another angle, this constant shifting meant that many new firms started up, and since Americans were inclined to overoptimistic and superficial assessments of risks, there were likewise many failures. Nathaniel Griswold said that, of a hundred New York City merchants he had known in the first half of the nineteenth century, only seven had completely avoided failure.[10] But since "failure" was largely a matter of shifting accounts, continuous new starts set a trend of innovation in the economy that more than conpensated for any stalling due to the temporary misallocation of money that resulted from insolvency.

The combination of two rapidly advancing cultures with a common language was a stimulant to technical progress in both Britain and America. Except during periods of war, immigrants (often illegal) from the British Isles were an important source for America of both labor and technical information. The linguistic compatibility between the cultures led to continuous movement of businessmen between the two nations, with many of the British coming to America to stay.

V

Culture is necessarily based on, although not always dominated by, geography. Industrialization might have first developed under relatively adverse geographical circumstances, but historically it did not. Furthermore, differing cultures, as illustrated by adjacent parts of France and Germany, may exist in areas quite similar geographically. Britain and the northeastern United States shared geographic environments highly favorable to industrialization. Both had fertile agricultural land, penetrated by many bays and rivers, and both had the types of natural resources needed for early mechanization. That a geographic interpretation cannot supersede a cultural interpretation, however, is illustrated by Japan, where an excellent geographic endowment did not lead to industrialization until cultural forces, specifically nationalism, demanded such development.

The general fertility of land and the trading advantages of coastal Britain and much of northeastern America had produced an agricultural and commercial society that by the late eighteenth century had a relatively high standard of living. Geography, that is, permitted a culture with a good margin of economic surplus that could be used for experiments in new methods and forms of production. It would be hard, by contrast, to imagine industrialization occurring in the minimal subsistence culture of Tierra del Fuego.

Geographic resources such as raw materials needed for expanded or new types of production obviously constitute another factor in development, but one that is not, as illustrated in phases of Japanese growth, a *sine qua non* on the same basic level as some of those already discussed. Coking coal close to iron was a major factor in Britain only after 1785 and was of no great importance before 1850 in the United States. If, however, the generalization is rephrased to say that abundant material for smelting and refining near to iron ore is a factor in development, it has a place in a generalized explanation. Until the mid-nineteenth century, the forests of the northeastern American seaboard produced plenty of fuel for processing iron ore and running steam engines, while scores of mill streams could produce power more cheaply than in Britain.

VI

Geography and culture, by helping to determine the types of local production and demand, affect business decisions and hence the directions of industrial progress. In general, the technical writings and workbench skills of the late eighteenth century were common throughout the Western world. English craftsmen, however, were taught high degrees of specialization, while those in America were prepared by necessity to do whatever they had to do. Fortunately, a civilization in which wood was superabundant allowed American bunglers to write off mistakes and push ahead. Meanwhile, traditional British skills frequently hindered attempts at new methods. Hence there is often little meaning in close comparisons of the journeys by the two cultures to mature industrialization. Given the state of Western world knowledge, either would have made rapid progress without the other, and, in spite of traditional writing to the contrary, their paths often diverged rather widely and fruitfully.

Among many diverse responses to different local demand, three examples will suffice. When an Arkwright water frame for spinning thread, often viewed as the most important early invention (1769) of the industrial revolution, was brought to Philadelphia in the 1780s it failed to attract local capital because its advantages in reducing costs in the local market seemed questionable. At the same time Oliver Evans's completely mechanized flour mills in Delaware did not seem worth the investment to British millers who, like the Philadelphia spinners, produced on a small scale for local demand rather than for export. Similarly, incorporated joint-stock banks gave a lift to development in land-rich but capital-hungry America from 1782 on, while in geographically stable and financially wealthy Britain private bank influence prevented such charters until 1825. Therefore, in cases of rapid development such as in Britain and America, differences in production based on local circumstances make it useless to speculate on who is ahead at any given time. With a relatively rapid interchange of knowledge and what came by the early nineteenth century to be near equality in practical skills, each nation led the way in meeting its own special needs and exploiting its own opportunities.

Thus even before the Revolution of 1776 American culture and geography had created an economy prepared to go forward faster than British imperial policy allowed. In this setting a new generation of entrepreneurs inspired by the post-Rovolutionary feeling of suddenly being free to do what they wanted made a rapid series of innovations. Being "free," of course, included freedom to influence new state governments to take the actions formerly denied by Britain. While factions fought each other and farmers opposed some of what the merchants desired, on the whole the new state governments were facilitators of business to a greater degree than any previous governments in history. When a strong federal government was established in 1789, it, too, became responsive to measures desired by the business community. In spite of their overwhelming majority among the population, farmers were generally represented in both state and federal legislatures by agri-businessmen, lawyers, or merchants. So that it may be said that from 1783 to the 1820s, the northeastern United States had a culture, including the instruments of government, as well as a geographic environment, uniquely stimulating to new economic activity.

Thus the lesson history gives to the developers of new regions is discouraging: the test of the virility of ongoing industrialization is not so much in the capital invested or the temporary volume of mechanized production as it is in the character of the processes that are attempted and their relation to the prople's abilities, purchasing power, and interests. This much has been recognized. A recent Saudi Arabian law attempts to stack the deck in favor of the natives by forbidding foreigners from owning small businesses while at the same time enabling a Saudi to "lend" his name in return for a share of the profits. The easiest methods for making money need only a signature. Obviously, in contrast to eighteenth-century America, this twentieth-century nation lacks confidence in the generative forces of its own culture and is reluctantly seeking aid that it expects will remain exotic.

2
A Business Basis
for Industrialization

The better houses, new machines, more varied clothing, and greater literacy that have marked the advent of "modern" American society came initially from a culture favoring a business elite interested in quicker, cheaper transportation and communication. The early forces on the frontiers of change were created by men who in expanding their markets or traveling on business affairs saw new things and accepted new ideas. Sometimes they saw, simply, better machines; more often they observed more efficient ways of conducting routine business.

Since the business system coordinates and implements the economic factors in society, its operation is of primary importance. The mobilization of savings through banks, insurance companies, and other means provides the capital necessary for the adoption of new technology or the improvement of services. The system of savings and their use is so interwoven between debtors and creditors, entrepreneurs and passive investors, advocates of change and their opponents, that it is sensitive to many types of "outside" pressures, both psychological and physical. Business collectively, therefore, may be said to have periods of optimism and pessimism, aggressive risk taking and cautious restraint. And as the business system also reflects the culture, it does not operate the same way in any two nations.

I

In the 1780s the early mills on the Brandywine in Delaware and the machine shops in southeastern Pennsylvania thrived as part of a dy-

namic trade area that I shall call, for the purposes of this study, the
Northeast Coast. Nowhere else in the world of 1800 were two cities as
big as New York and Philadelphia only eighty miles apart and brought
into close contact by waterways and level terrain. Furthermore, they
were only the center of a longer chain of cities from Baltimore to Providence and Boston that under the influence of America's commitment to
business vied with each other in new devices and ideas. Of the two big
Middle States cities, New York became more important as a seaport,
Philadelphia as the major center for assembling raw materials and developing heavy industry, while both, along with the other urban centers, manufactured lighter goods for many of the same markets. The
rapidly growing cities on the Northeast Coast were stimulated at first by
exchanges with their own hinterlands and later by an increasing movement of men and goods among them. This pattern of urban growth goes
far toward explaining the speed of American economic development.

While cities connected by water dotted the entire Northeast Coast,
the character of the backcountry regions that traded with the principal
seaports varied in ways that significantly affected their economic character. New England was really two regions: a coastal one from southern
Maine to the Connecticut shoreline on Long Island Sound that offered
good water transportation and fast-flowing rivers for mills and had a relatively dense population, and the backcountry parts of Maine and Massachusetts, New Hampshire and Vermont, where isolated farmers were
at first little affected by the quickening of commercial life along the
seacoast.

Likewise the Middle States, if one includes Delaware, Maryland,
New Jersey, Pennsylvania, and New York, shared characteristics of good
water transportation near the coast, sparse population over the area as a
whole, localities with good waterpower, and sections of rich soil. But
they also break down into diverse subregions. The Mohawk Valley of
upstate New York had fertile soil, and, when a canal about a mile long
around the Little Falls opened in 1796, its farm products could go by
water to New York City. Thus the city with the best port came to be
connected by waterways with a backcountry as extensive as that of eastern Pennsylvania. New Jersey was really three regions: a hilly, moderately fertile one just north of the main routes from New York City to
Philadelphia; a rather narrow, flat farming area starting at the Delaware
River near Philadelphia and Wilmington and crossing the state from
Trenton to Newark; and finally a vast stretch of pine barrens and thin

soil that covered the whole southern part of the state. As can readily be imagined, the areas near New York City and Philadelphia quickly developed industry and improved agriculture, while the southern part of the state stagnated.

Baltimore, while fifty miles farther from the sea than Philadelphia, was more easily reached by sailing ships coming from the south. The city also could draw lumber and farm products from central Pennsylvania down the shallow and treacherous Susquehanna River that entered Chesapeake Bay about fifty miles to the north. In addition to tobacco and wheat, neraby Maryland and Virginia had depostis of bituminous coal and iron. Yet, for all its advantages, Baltimore lacked the potential hinterland of either New York or Philadelphia.[1] The lower Chesapeake Bay and the broad, gently flowing rivers of Virginia, which could be navigated by seagoing vessels, made transshipment of imports largely unnecessary.

As the business basis for new development was improved in the years after the Revolution, the most important overall regional factors in the growth of the Middle States were three major ports within a space of less than two hundred miles overland, the opportunity for protected water communication, an established commercial network, and rapid inmigration to the cities. In all, it was an environment highly favorable to growth.

In contrast, south of Maryland many factors worked against rapid industrial development. The Southeast Coast lacked major river systems that would determine mandatory points for transshipment. The seventeenth-century decision to use slave labor for agriculture induced free white immigrants to head for the northern ports. As a result, white labor in the seaboard South was scarce and expensive. Carville V. Earle and Ronald A. Hoffman hold that staple crop agriculture, whether tobacco, rice, sugar, or cotton, does not encourage the growth of regional manufacturing centers.[2] From the standpoint of the argument of this book, another powerful factor retarding development in the South was an elitist culture that did not reward the skilled innovator or the rising manufacturer. The road to social and political prestige was ownership of plantations and slaves. Large aggregations of laborers—whether in mines or in factories, whether black or white—caused many problems and were not welcomed by the rulers of a system built around the export of staple crops produced by slave labor.[3]

Industry grew up on the river systems West of the Appalachians, but

well after the industrial revolution had occurred along the Northeast
Coast. Prior to the 1830s western cities such as Pittsburgh, Cincinnati,
and Cleveland developed local industries with both capital and technology supplied from the East. The volume of East-West trade however,
was small compared to the local trade of the Northeast.

II

It seems idle to speculate whether specialization in business practices or
faster transportation and communication were more important in paving the way for industrialization. In the United States business changes
came first; in Britain improvements in transportation and business
methods went on side by side over a considerably longer period. In both
nations the large seaport merchant of the mid-eighteenth century imported and exported, transported and warehoused, sold wholesale and
retail, lent money and arranged for investments, both sought and subscribed to insurance, and was a man to consult about all matters of
business. He might specialize on certain trades, such as the West Indian
or Anglo-American, but generally not on special business functions.
Except when owning or chartering ships, his labor force was minuscule.
One or two clerks and a porter might be the only office employees of a
substantial merchant. This skeleton organization could function ade-
quately only because volume was small and time expendable. Needless
to add, again except for ships, fixed capital was also small and the chief
cost was granting credit to customers and carrying inventories far larger
in relation to turnover than would be the case in later years. In other
words, aside from ships, working capital was the chief overhead cost.

Hence the beginnings of change often came from efforts to econo-
mize on the cost of renting money. One way was to make funds available where and when needed, on a basis more flexible than possible
with the assets of a single family. In late eighteenth-century England individuals who regularly accumulated excess capital often lent funds to
merchants; a prosperous brewer, for example, might set up as a private
banker. In America, where there was much less old wealth and a greater
demand for improvements, the chartered banks from 1780 on were a
means of mobilizing the savings of a large number of individuals for
loans that would facilitate trade. To a certain degree merchants in the
United States pulled themselves up by their own bootstraps. When trade
was relatively slack from 1783 to 1789, some merchants had capital
beyond that which they thought wise to commit to trading ventures. By

buying stock in a bank they could get higher and more secure returns on their money than by keeping it in their own business. So merchants became both the chief stockholders in the seaport banks, and ultimately the chief borrowers.

III

Chartered commercial banks not only marked a major financial innovation on a worldwide frontier of change but also illustrated one of the new concepts of American law: the use of incorporation for all types of business. It had never been clear in the colonial period whether or not governors had the power to charter private business or utility corporations, and very few had been created. The British attorney general never got around to ruling on their legality. After the Revolution, New Haven and Boston wharf companies, three Rhode Island water companies, and a fire insurance company in Philadelphia were the only active corporate businesses surviving from the colonial period.[4]

Corporations had been chartered by sovereign governments since Roman times, at least, but traditionally they were subagencies of government set up to manage communities or necessary public works. In the early Republic all the state legislatures made use of this function of sovereignty and expanded the concept of public welfare to include chartering all types of businesses. While charters took some lobbying, particularly when there were conflicting interests seeking action, a great many were granted as legislatures were small and contained many members themselves involved in business promotions. In New York, the fastest growing state, there were 220 incorporations between 1800 and 1810.[5] This ready use of the corporation, in contrast to Europe where only sizable public works could secure charters, and then only with much difficulty, appears to have been one of the major factors in the rapid American development.

Ease of incorporation should not cast too warm a light, however, on the supportive character of law in general for economic development in the post-Revolutionary years. The most pervasive favorable factor in law, as in other institutions, was the culture itself, with its traditional bias toward the entrepreneur, or the person engaged in buying and selling. On the unfavorable side, after 1789, were the often conflicting statutes and judicial interpretations of nearly a score of states and an untested federal jurisdiction. Had a truly national business system arisen from the confused years of the Confederation, discrepancies and uncer-

tainties in the law could have seriously retarded growth. But a movement toward a national business system was not the direction taken on
the frontiers of change. Rather each major port city in the Northeast developed an increasingly intensive intraregional network, generally involving only two or three neighboring states.[6] More distant trade was
generally conducted through reliable agents, as it had been in the colonial period, and the uncertainties of interstate legal actions do not seem
to have been a serious hindrance.

Aiding the businessman were the judges in both state and federal
courts. They were likely to be local farming or commercial entrepreneurs favorable to business development. While all the state legislatures
had some factions that sought to hold up charters or force the passage of
statutes unfavorable to some business operations, such squabbles represented, on the whole, warfare between groups that differed merely in
their conceptions of development. To ease these situations the federal
courts, set up in 1789, tried with varying success to extend their jurisdiction in the interest of greater uniformity.[7] In any case, interregional
trade was relatively unimportant to early industrial growth in the United
States, and so the disparate structure of the new nation's legal system
was not as much of a hindrance to business as it might at first seem
when compared to the operation of a legal system in a more unified
country like Great Britain. Furthermore, American judges were often
ready to cast aside common law precedents that interfered with efficient
development. During the early years of the Republic the changes in
American institutions, whether economic, social, or political, were
greatly influenced by the interaction of judges and legislatures favorable
to what they conceived to be economic progress.[8]

At the time of their independence the American states passed "reception" laws specifying the British statutes or decisions they regarded as in
effect. Most of the states also allowed for equity jurisdiction in cases for
which neither statute nor common law provided for justice. In all of
this hasty legislation, together with the wholesale appointment of new
justices, the authority of common law precedents became unclear or
unknown. As a result, judges largely remade the common law in the interest of business or economic necessities, and in so doing inevitably
came to regard themselves as legislators. For example, in *Thurston v. Koch*
(1803) a Pennsylvania judge held that it was better to distribute losses
among many creditors than to ruin a few entrepreneurs. In 1814 the

Pennsylvania chief justice, Henry Brackenridge, condemned judges who bound themselves by precedents as fearful of innovation.[9] During his nine years as chancellor of New York (1814–23), James Kent said he never heard an opinion of one of his predecessors cited.[10]

Some traditional practices, however, helped to soften the adverse effect inconsistent state or federal decisions might have had on business. Two such carryovers from the English past into the period after 1780 were mercantile law and the jurisdiction of chancery (equity) courts. Mercantile law, often involving actions by foreigners, had developed outside the English common law, but during the eighteenth century its doctrines were taken over by the regular British courts. In America, however, businessmen in the chief commercial states could still appeal to mercentile arbitration tribunals instead of to the courts for decisions on questions of credit, property rights, and liabilities. Not until 1807 were such tribunals abolished in New York, the chief trading state, and their functions taken over by the courts. The practice persisted elsewhere, but after 1830 the jurisdiction of these tribunals was limited to a preliminary hearing.[11]

Equity—the placing of justice ahead of doctrine—became in the hands of American lawyers and jurists a means of upsetting or avoiding jury verdicts hostile, often from ignorance, to the needs of business. Consequently chancery courts were frequently regarded by backcountry factions as undemocratic, and by the 1840s equity was being absorbed into the common law. In many states, however, judges still exercised the power to set jury verdicts aside and hold new trials.

In the 1820s growing intercity trade and a greater need for roads and canals, plus varied questions of liability, were producing new legal problems. As Morton J. Horwitz has observed, "Law was no longer thought of as an eternal set of principles expressed in custom and derived from natural law."[12] Often the judge thought more in terms of what was best for society, and his thinking had a strong bias toward the economic and expedient. Or perhaps one should say that in reviewing novel situations the judge tried to think in these terms. Among the new technologies demanding legal controls were improvements in transportation. Only Vermont, Massachusetts, and Pennsylvania required compensation for damages caused by a turnpike, bridge, or canal corporation exercising the eminemt domain provided for in its charter, chiefly because the problem had seldom arisen before the trunpike era. To relieve the courts of such cases without precedent Pennsylvania, New York, New Jersey, Maryland, Ohio, and North Carolina ultimately provided for local commissions to assess damages.

Of all the problems that grew from the system of conflicting state and federal sovereignties, none was more universal and intricate than that of "negotiable" instruments—the "commercial paper" or bills due from one businessman to another. According to late eighteenth-century English common law, to be "negotiable"—that is, to circulate and be legally binding on the debtor—a bill had to (1) be drawn up in the normal course of business (not in order to pay some previous debt), (2) involve some current and valuable consideration, and (3) have been accepted by the holder with faith that the first two conditions prevailed. A note was said to be "accepted" when a third party took it from the holder or drawer and added a second signature, indicating that he took responsibility for collection.[13] In a typical transaction a planter might write a note on a New York merchant who owed him money for cotton and a local "factor," or middleman, in a southern city would endorse the note, putting his local credit behind that of the drawer and debtor. The endorsement gave the bill the status of "negotiable" currency or "commercial paper." In New York City the bill could also pass from hand to hand on the basis of the credit of the local merchant (debtor) as well as that of the southern middleman.[14]

Legal problems arose when a bill was presented to the debtor (payee) and refused because of some defect in the note. The trouble could range from outright fraud (no such sum being due the planter), and down through a range of various technicalities (such as an assertion that the note did not arise in the normal course of business). The states had varying laws regarding negotiability, which might prevent collection by creditors from out of state. Again, had interregional trade been the chief developmental force, the differences among states in interpreting negotiability could have been a serious impediment to industrialization, but since in the early years such trade was both limited in type and long established, the merchants involved knew what to expect.

The hindrance to some businesses was strong enough, however, to lead the federal courts to play a role in litigation over negotiablity. In *Coolidge v. Payson* (1817) the United States Supreme Court held a note negotiable even though drawn to pay a previous debt, in other words, a debt not arising in the normal course of business. But in local cases the courts did not have to be bound by federal decisions, and they were not.

From Independence through the 1840s the state laws regarding negotiable instruments continued to vary. The many bankruptcies before and following the panic of 1837 led federal courts to seek to extend their jurisdiction in interstate cases granted by Section 34 of the Judiciary Act of 1789. In *Swift v. Tyson* (1842) the Supreme Court ruled that within the federal sphere there existed a uniform common law, including that affecting negotiable instruments.[15] But even a greater willingness on the part of the federal courts to accept cases in "diversity" (interstate) jurisdiction could not cure the lack of uniformity, and differences from one state to another remained numerous in the 1840s.[16]

The same contradictions or uncertainties that superficially, at least, harassed interstate trade in negotiable instruments also affected the collection of other debts. Bankruptcy and insolvency laws and practices varied from state to state, and to add to the confusion the Constitution gave Congress the power to pass general bankruptcy laws. But, again, the legal jungle was not as threatening to the aspiring entrepreneur as it might seem. An increase in leniency toward debtors was desired by both business lenders and borrowers, and where the laws were the most lenient, as in New York, by 1820 "the haven for debtors," economic progress was the most rapid of anywhere in the nation. While no close correlation is claimed, this coincidence of leniency toward debtors and rapid development suggests, at the least, that the state and federal disagreements over bankruptcy were not major barriers to economic progress.

As business risks increased in England in the late eighteenth century, a fundamental distinction was made between bankruptcy, which applied to debts contracted for business purposes, and insolvency, which applied to personal delinquency.[17] But of the laws existing in the American states, only the Pennsylvania bankruptcy statute of 1785 specifically limited application to "merchants, scriveners, bankers, brokers, or factors."[18] This type of law reassured risk-taking entrepreneurs, but it did nothing for those imprisoned on account of personal insolvency. Their problems, not so directly concerned with economic growth, were relegated to the realm of humanitarian social reform.

In general the Revolution did not alter the common law approach to the relations of debtors and creditors. Imprisonment was the rule in all states. Peter J. Coleman estimates that "in the early nineteenth century one householder in every five would, during his working life-time, fail outright rather than merely default on a particular debt. The incidence of difficulty probably rose as the century advanced." Laws abolishing imprisonment for debt did not come until the rise of workingmen's parties in the 1830s, but for the business debtor there were an increasing number of ways for avoiding jail. Between 1776 and 1810, with differences in detail, Connecticut, Georgia, Maryland, Massachusetts, New Jersey, New York, Pennsylvania, and Virginia allowed debtors to exchange their property for freedom from prison.[19] By adroit assignment of property to trusted family members in advance of default, the debtor might lose very little.

In 1800 Congress finally enacted a national bankruptcy law, but one liked by neither debtors nor creditors, and it was repealed in 1803.[20] It was not possible to get congressional agreement on another act until 1841, but meanwhile the federal judiciary confused the issue by a circuit court ruling in *Golden v. Prince* (1814) that the federal power over bankruptcy was exclusive, followed by a very confusing Supreme Court decision in *Sturgis v. Crowninshield* (1819) upholding a New York law of 1811. Finally in *Odgen v. Saunders* (1827) the Supreme Court validated a New York bankruptcy law for debts contracted after its passage.[21]

The connection between bankruptcy and business progress is demonstrated by New York, the fastest growing state and after 1811 the leading state in granting relief for debtors. Pennsylvania, the other economic leader, as well as neighboring New Jersey, moved in general agreement with the rulings of New York and paid little heed to the uncertainties of federal decisions. Regional legal uniformity again emphasizes the importance of the central area of American industrialization comprised of Delaware, New Jersey, New York, and Pennsylvania. In contrast, Massachusetts, perhaps because of the strength of mercantile creditors, passed no state bankruptcy law until 1838, and its court decisions were generally stricter than those of neighboring Connecticut or New York.[22]

Obviously the business cycle was closely related to defaults and insolvency. When sharp entrepreneurs judged a boom to be near the peak, they secretly assigned their good properties and defaulted on their borrowings. Hence the number of defaults peaked before, not after, panics.[23] Following panics many states enacted "stay laws," postponing sales of property for satisfaction of debts until prices again became normal.

The deep depression following the panic of 1837 and the chaotic condition of state laws led President Van Buren to recommend a national bankruptcy law confined to banks. In the four years of congressional debate that followed, business-minded conservatives, like Daniel Webster in the Senate, expressed themselves in favor of a bill providing for both voluntary and involuntary bankruptcy for all classes of debtors including corporations. Joseph Story, associate justice of the Supreme Court, drafted such a bill, but it had difficulty securing a majority in either house. Some mercantile creditor areas in the Northeast as well as some planters from the Southeast opposed release of debtors through bankruptcy; strict constructionists and states rights advocates believed federal action, particularly if applied to corporations, unconstitutional; and finally the presidential request was, of course, labeled as Democratic and therefore to be opposed by many Whigs. Thus, in spite of the need for uniform bankruptcy legislation recognized by farsighted businessmen, during nearly four years nothing was accomplished.[24]

In August of 1841, about the worst period of the long depression lasting from 1837 to 1843, Congress finally passed a Whig-sponsored bill that provided for both voluntary and involuntary bankruptcy but excluded corporations. The act remained in force only a little over a year, but 34,000 persons with $441 million in debts took advantage of its provisions.[25] It is a testimony to both the foresight of the entrepreneurs and the severity of the depression that the debtors surrendered property worth less than 10 percent of their indebtness. With the return of prosperity in 1843, pressure for new federal or state action died down, not to be revived until after the panic of 1857.[26]

Meanwhile, state-enacted stay laws, exempting parts of a debtor's property from execution, and the gradual limitation of imprisonment for debt had been meeting the most pressing problems of personal insolvency. These laws came mainly in the major depression periods, such as 1784–87, 1807–09, 1818–22, and 1837–43. The usual function of stay laws was to prevent the sale of property by foreclosure for a certain period of time unless it brought one-half to three-quarters of its appraised value. The early laws exempting certain types of property from liens were the results of demands by labor leaders for protection of workers' tools; later laws also exempted dwellings of low value and certain amounts of farm acreage from seizure to satisfy general, as opposed to specific or chattel mortgage, indebtness.[27]

In the period from 1780 to 1850, contracts and debts had become increasingly impersonal. To the extent that debt was represented by bank loans, mortgages, or notes accepted by a third party, there might be no personal acquaintance between borrower and lender. As transportation opened new possibilities of development, Americans probably became more attuned to speculation and the salvation, if necessary, of recourse to the law. Coleman writes, "It would possibly be a bit much to say that every American was a latent robber baron . . . [although] the pendulum of opinion swung from hostility to bankruptcy relief to an attitude that mixed indifference with tolerance and outright approval." [28] Implied in this comment is the generally accepted hypothesis that cultural change is gradual, that the manipulation of the law in favor of development had a long genesis before it became so obvious in the later nineteenth century.

IV

In effect, large and even fraudulent defaulters mobilized community savings to finance development projects at the expense of the creditors. Corporations accomplished the same end by the sale of their stock or bonds not only to savers but also to governments and banks. Pre-Revolutionary entrepreneurs like Robert Morris had seen the advantages of joint-stock banks for creating capital and allowing mercantile lending, but British controls prevented such organizations. Consequently the first American bank was not chartered until 1780, when New York and Philadelphia merchants set up an emergency credit organization to finance Congress's military purchases. It was never a true commercial bank, and its affairs were liquidated in 1784.

Meanwhile a new corporation was chartered in 1781 and 1782 by the Continental Congress and the commonwealth of Pennsylvania, respectively, as the Bank of North America (BNA). With the war still going on, the promoters had difficulty in raising the $400,000 in specie that was required in the charter. As both a leading incorporator of the bank and the superintendent of finance of the Confederation, Robert Morris subscribed $254,000 in French specie to pay for the government's share of the stock and then immediately borrowed the money for public use. Advancing specie, borrowing it back, and later paying off the loan in paper was a practice also common among individual subscribers. In 1782 Connecticut, Rhode Island, New York, and Massachusetts formally endorsed Congress's action in chartering a bank, and, with the legal support of these chief business states, the BNA seemed secure.

But in 1785 a Pennsylvania backcountry faction attacked the BNA, secured passage of a law to set up an office to lend up to £50,000 on

farm mortgages, and in September of that year was successful in repeal-
ing the bank's charter. Delaware responded by granting the BNA a
charter in February 1786. In the following months Morris, by now an
awe-inspiring figure, led a movement in the Pennsylvania Senate for
recharter. Recongnizing that farmers needed long-term credit, Morris
also favored the state loan office supported by the backcountry faction.
In the widespread debates on the social and economic services of banks,
the strongest public support for the BNA came from newspaper articles
by the chief propagandist of the Revolution, Thomas Paine. In the next
election the pro-BNA forces secured enough support to reenact the
charter in March 1787 and temporarily put to rest the issue of state
lending.

The well-administered Philadelphia bank served as a model for similar New York and Boston corporations. At the start the BNA was the
only chartered bank in the world run exclusively for profit to the stockholders, and its president Thomas Willing, a former partner of Robert
Morris, was necessarily on a frontier of change. At the request of William Phillips and other promoters of the Massachusetts bank he wrote a
letter, not only revealing as to the source of operating practices but also
containing one of the early applications of the word *science* to commerce. "I am too much a Citizen of the World," he wrote, "to wish to
confine this Useful Science of Business to any Particular Spot or Set of
Men. . . . When the bank was first opened here, the business . . .
was a pathless wilderness. . . . In this situation we adopted the only
safe method to avoid confusion. Educated as merchants . . . we established our books on a simple mercantile plan, and this mode . . . has
carried us through, so far without a material loss or even a mistake of
any consequence." [29] The carryover of mercantile methods into banking
meant investment in accommodation loans or discounts and drafts on
London correspondents. Documentary bills (notes covering goods in
transit or inventory), domestic drafts, and acceptances (negotiable bills)
became of major importance in the seaport city portfolios only in the
1820s. Operating in its early days with old-fashioned practices on this
new financial frontier, Willing's bank made 14 percent profit in 1783
and in 1784. [30]

New York had the same contending factions as Pennsylvania. Various upcountry groups wanted either a bank with two-thirds of its capital
in land or banking by the state through the printing and lending of
notes. With help from Alexander Hamilton, the inflationists were held

at bay, and a group of the more prominent New York merchants organized a joint-stock bank. It is interesting that both the first president and the cashier were Scots by birth, although not trained in that advanced center of eighteenth-century banking. The president, General Alexander McDougal, had been a member of the radical Sons of Liberty before the Revolution as well as a high officer in the Continental Army, while the cashier, William Seton, had worked with the British during the occupation of New York. Such healing of Revolutionary antagonisms in the interest of postwar business were frequent all over the nation, but particularly so in New York City, where a revived chamber of commerce embraced men from each faction. But back-country continued to be pitted against port city in a rift that perhaps has never been cured. Although the New York bank did a profitable business from 1784 on, the country representatives in the New York legislature prevented the granting of a charter until 1791.

Unlike New York and Philadelphia, Boston had no serious legislative problems in securing a charter for a bank in 1784. Willing's letter to William Phillips and five other promoters was, as in the case of New York, followed by a visit of the Massachusetts cashier to the Philadelphia bank. Like the other pioneers, the Massachusetts bank was well run and made money. Baltimore, the other major city in the Northeast, was hampered by political antagonisms and a smaller business community and did not establish a bank until 1791.

If a "modern or managerial corporation" is defined as one in which directors and managers collectively own less than a majority of the stock, all three pioneer banks and most of the later ones fall into this category. Shares costing $400 or $500 were widely distributed, and average holdings consisted of only two or three shares. The New York bank sought to prevent control by small group with a system for diminishing the voting power of the larger holdings. Holdings of five to seven shares had only five votes, holdings of eight shares had six, and holdings of ten shares had seven, originally the maximum. A later amendment to the corporate statutes allowed one vote for each additional five shares above ten.[31]

Restraints on voting power call attention to the need for early incorporators to respect the democratic ideas proclaimed by their agrarian opponents. On the surface, corporations seemed compatible with democracy. Granted a charter by vote of a democratic legislature, the corporation was run by a board of directors selected by a "democratic" voting of its shares. That difficulties in attending stockholders meetings and lack of information regarding the affairs of the company prevented control by the majority in practically all large corporations should not obscure the initial concept of a corporation as a democracy of small stockholders.

In each city the original bank tried to prevent the chartering of competitors, and in each case it failed. One reason was that legislators found the incorporation of banks financially rewarding. Pennsylvania demanded that the state be given bank stock in return for a charter. By 1810 the commonwealth owned 7,634 shares, worth $2 million, and the dividends paid the expenses of state government.[32] Cash payments to the states for charters were also demanded. New York, for example, made the City Bank pay $120,000 into the Common School Fund in return for its charter in 1812. Forcing banks to invest in state-financed transportation companies was another common practice.[33]

The seaport banks could carry on an essentially mercantile business and follow traditional rules for financial "soundness." Their loans were short term, their customers tended to be financially sound, and their note issues were well protected by paid-in capital. In the language of banking history, these banks operated on the "real bills" principle, one in which liquidity was assured by adequate short-term assets. As chartered banks spread into the backcountry, however, they had to operate differently. Here the chief assets were not claims on the accounts of merchants but rather on farms, buildings, machinery, and crops. Bank currency was needed to stimulate growth, and loans could not be backed exclusively or even chiefly by short-term notes. Started by potential borrowers, the banks assumed some of the capital burden of community development. Collectively they made a considerable contribution, and the fact that nearly half of those that opened between 1810 and 1820 had failed by 1825 was not as serious as it may sound.[34] The physical improvements remained, and only a group of entrepreneurs and stockholders lost money. From what little can be learned, it seems that the ups and downs of the business cycle affected prices, solvency, and credit more than real production. Richard Sylla judges that "credit creation, rather than distorting resource allocation may well have served to improve it."[35]

By means of bank credit, inland entrepreneurs in trade, construction, and manfacturing drew on the resources of the port cities for additional cash. The tendency of country banks was to issue and lend printed notes for several times the amount of the nominal capital of the bank, much of which might not have been paid in. The effect, of course, was inflationary, but this inflation was not necessarily bad. Without it, shortage of cash would have slowed down the volume of business transactions. Such banks were on a frontier of change unique to the United States. They were testing, far more than European country banks could or did, the lending limits beyond which it was unsafe to go, limits that in succeeding years would be defined by state regulations and ultimately by the federal government.

In spite of nearly eighty chartered banks by 1810, most capital for fixed investment was still being transferred from savers to users without going through financial intermediaries of any type.[36] Mortgaging by direct negotiation between borrower and lender was no doubt the principal form of borrowing or investing for capital formation. But it should be continually borne in mind that, except for building construction and transportation, early industrialization was not capital intensive, rather national economic growth came chiefly from business and agricultural efficiency and the application of technological skills to relatively low-cost innovations. The metalworking innovations of Nathan Sellers or Oliver Evans from 1780 to 1815 did not require large initial investments, although if the latter had had access to substantial capital steam locomotives might have appeared twenty years earlier.

V

From 1791 to 1811 and again from 1816 to 1836, practical limitations on the issuing of bank currency were imposed by the Bank of the United States (BUS). During the presidency of the aged and experienced Willing, who left his post at the BNA to head the BUS, the federal bank, with branches in all the chief commercial centers, could check the overissue of notes by collecting a large number of them and then presenting them for redemption in specie to the outraged cashiers of recklessly expanded banks. Both this practice, and the fact that the branches of the BUS did commercial banking with many advantages over other institutions in the transfer of funds and in providing foreign and interregional exchange, made it unpopular with almost all local bankers. Consequently, when the first bank's recharter came up in Congress in 1811, it was narrowly defeated by a coalition of back-country representatives opposed to all banking interests and a few representatives from New York jealous of the financial strength the BUS brought to Philadelphia.

The demise of the BUS called national attention to the most successful American financier of the early period, Stephen Girard. The son of one of the local political leaders of Bordeaux, he immigrated to Philadelphia and from the 1780s on accumulated a fortune by meticulously careful and intelligent trading. With relations between Britain and the United States becoming strained, this slight, unemotional, humorless Frenchman had Baring Brothers, his London agents, move money from his European credit balances into shares of the BUS. When the bank was not rechartered, he took over the successful liquidation of its ample assets, for which he was the chief claimant.[37]

That an individual merchant was able to buy the bank's massively columned head office on Chestnut Street together with its accounts and start a private bank is an indication of the wealth that had accrued to many such men in the great trade boom before 1808 and had given the United States a small number of sound and experienced merchant bankers whose personal notes passed as currency. One of the earliest of these, Thomas Biddle, was operating in Philadelphia before the Revolution. After 1800 chartered banks became numerous and these corporations were able to get their state legislatures to forbid private issue of bank notes. Massachusetts and New Hampshire did so in 1799, New York in 1804, and other states followed between then and 1820. Some of the private bankers secured charters, but others went on doing their business through certificates of deposit and personal bills. Girard's lawyers, among the best in the nation, made the courts fearful of forbidding an individual the right to issue his own personal notes. Hence while the Philadelphia banks joined with those in the Pennsylvania backcountry in securing passage of state laws in 1811 and 1816 that restricted note issue by private banks, Girard's personal notes were not interfered with. Finally, in 1816, when the state and the banks of Philadelphia wanted to return to a specie basis and needed Girard's help, his notes were accepted.

Philadelphia's troubles illustrate one aspect of the financial chaos in the states south of New England from 1812 to 1816. The War of 1812 was entered into despite the vote of the Northeast Coast, and the nearly solid opposition of New England—in other words, against the will of the principal commercial and financial interests. Both Congress and the secretary of the treasury, Albert Gallatin, thought the war could be financed by loans. But with little support from the financial community, that proved impossible. In the beginning the help of leading merchants like John Jacob Astor and Girard, together with some European aid,

made a large loan moderately successful, but subsequently the treasury
was reduced to selling bonds far below par and finally to financing by
short-term notes. The capture of Washington by the British in 1814 led
to suspension of specie payments south of New England. New England
itself, with a regional surplus in balance of payments and a lack of interest in the war, was able to maintain finance as usual.

As early as 1814 Astor and Girard recognized that financial salvation
for both the government and the key Middle States region required a
new national bank. Political jockeying and relatively weak secretaries of
the treasury delayed a final charter until 1816, by which time the government was living from hand to mouth by the continuous issue and
renewal of short-term notes. The whole situation was reminiscent of
1781 and also demonstrated that Gallatin's theory of long-term governmental affluence was not a guarantee against short-term needs.

The Second Bank of the United States was ultimately to be a part of
perhaps the best banking system the country has ever had. Once a bank
was agreed upon, the Philadelphia location created no great resistance.
One might wonder why the new BUS was not placed in New York, the
chief trade center. Perhaps the vulnerability of a seacoast city to naval
attack was still strong in some legislators' minds. One of the Upstate
New York representatives in Congress agreed to Philadelphia because it
was "a place of greater security and greater wealth . . . more central to
the commercial transactions and wealth of the country."[38] Perhaps
there was already regional jealousy of the growing power of New York
City.

Allowing for the increase in the nation's volume of business and for
the decline in the value of the dollar, the $35 million capital of the sec-
ond bank was proportionately the same as the $10 million subscribed to
the first bank in 1791. The government initially bought $10 million of
the capital stock, and Girard subscribed to (underwrote) the $3 million
necessary to complete the funding. Since he ultimately sold most of
these shares to his depositors and other business associates, the transaction shows the movement of private bankers toward the business of distributing securities from which was to grow investment banking.

After a period of loose management that helped create an inflation
collapsing in 1819 and an over stringent policy from then until 1822,
Nicholas Biddle of Philadelphia was made president of the BUS and followed much the same course that Willing had initiated some thirty
years earlier. The bank and its branches specialized in providing exchange rather than competing with the state banks in local credit. Its

ability to submit large quantities of bank notes for redemption in specie forced the state banks into reasonably conservative lending policies.

VI

There were other financial developments that fostered industrial growth. A relatively unimportant addition to bank credit came during the postwar period from the organization of savings funds or societies. These had become popular in England and Scotland primarily as philanthropic enterprises coaxing members of the lower class to save money. By 1815 George Rose's *Observations on Banks for Savings* and Henry Duncan's *Essay on the Nature and Advantages of Parish Banks*, as well as other British banking literature, were being read in the United States.[39] The popularity of this literature probably accounts for the nearly simultaneous movements in Boston, New York, and Philadelphia to establish savings banks. By commencing in December 1816 without waiting for a charter, the Philadelphia Saving Fund Society was the first to go into operation. It was quickly followed by others in major cities, and ultimately the state legislatures granted charters. During the first decade of operation the deposits in these banks provided a modest amount of additional funds for mortgages and government security issues.

Insurance companies were far more important financial intermediaries for pooling savings than such associations. A mutual fire insurance company was established in Philadelphia by Benjamin Franklin in 1752. By 1790 the idea of fire insurance by corporations was spreading rapidly in the port cities. In 1800 there were thirty-three chartered insurance companies in the nation, more of them in New England than in New York or Pennsylvania.[40] Immediately important in view of the trade boom of the 1790s was proper organization of marine casualty. In earlier years such insurance was arranged by posting descriptions of ships and voyages in coffee houses and soliciting individual subscriptions. A few wealthy merchants specialized in insurance, but they would seldom individually underwrite more than £200. Consequently insuring a voyage was an arduous and not always successful operation.

In 1792 the Insurance Company of North America in Philadelphia was organized to write both fire and marine insurance. In 1794 it was incorporated, as was a new competitor, the Insurance Company of the State of Pennsylvania. By 1800 similar companies, usually underwriting both fire and marine insurance, were operating in all the major port cities. These companies facilitated the speed of business by saving the insured a considerable amount of time and risk and by making capital available for investment from their mounting reserves.

In the early days there seems to have been little difference in the types of investment undertaken by insurance companies and banks. Both lent on personal notes, granted mortgages, and bought securities. Unfortunately, it is impossible to compare the amount of credit made available during this period by the various types of intermediaries, but the total picture is one of the United States, much more than in any other nation, using the corporation as a means of pooling savings in the interest of more efficient business, finance for all types of construction, and resulting economic growth.

Another increase in efficiency achieved through specialization came as trained bookkeepers supplanted all-purpose clerks in the making of ledger entries. The first American bookkeeping text was prepared by William Mitchell in Philadelphia in 1796, and within a dozen years it attracted imitators in New England and New York.[41] By explaining double entry, profit and loss accounts, and periodic balancing, Mitchell made it possible for the merchant to know his financial status at a glance and quickly evaluate the wisdom of some new risk. How much immediate influence these texts had is hard to guess. Corporations may have quickly adopted new methods, but merchants tended to continue familiar practices.[42]

VII

By 1800 banks both chartered and private, insurance companies, and specialized services were creating a national money market. Philadelphia, the national capital and precocious center of the 1790s, organized the first stock exchange. Soon brokers in Boston who traded in securities established regular hours and meeting places, and in New York they met at a certain buttonwood tree on Wall Street. In 1792 there was some lively trading in BUS shares, but until 1812 stock trading in general languished. Only Philadelphia had an organized exchange, and some brokers gave it up as not worth the time. By 1814, however, inflation was producing a larger and more speculative market in bank and transportation stocks plus state and federal bonds. The increased volume led a group of twenty New York traders in 1817 to set up an organized stock exchange closely modeled on that of Philadelphia.[43]

Selling negotiable commercial paper on commission was called note or bill brokerage. Such operations formed a very important part of the

British money market. By 1800 bill sellers were active in the major American port cities and particularly in Philadelphia, where markets generally set the rates of exchange. These brokers were often the same men who dealt in stocks and bonds. In 1806 the Philadelphia Domestic Society was chartered to lend on, and help dispose of, inventories. In spite of the legal uncertainties already discussed, backcountry trade grew and more southern bills based on cotton shipments appeared, especially in the Boston and New York City markets. As the volume of commercial paper increased, bill brokers became prominent and trusted businessmen, often combining note dealing with other forms of brokerage or private banking.[44]

It is easy to take a too-gloomy view of the early United States money market's efficiency in relation to that of England. In mid-century Walter Bagehot, the well-known London financial analyst, favored the American pattern of unit banks with individual responsibility to that of the British branch system legalized in 1825. As long as they were kept from large overissue of notes by a strong central bank, the American banks represented credit creation geared to supposed local needs. Although state jurisdictions made the American commercial paper or bill market more uncertain than the highly centralized British market based on London, the essentially intraregional basis of industrial trade made bills on distant payers, aside from cotton notes, relatively unimportant up to the 1820s. Whereas in London bill brokers, soon to become "discount houses," bought and sold bills on the interior and discounted them at the Bank of England, American brokers generally handled bills on a commission basis, thereby limiting themselves as financial intermediaries. In neither country at this time was there a reliable "secondary" market for the disposal of mortgages.

In all, with a central bank, widespread state banks, insurance company reserves, and connected urban money markets, America's credit facilities seemed to be keeping abreast of the needs of her developing economy. Each decade saw new institutions joining with technology itself in reducing the risks and costs of innovation and expansion. Not only was there the necessary financial and corporate apparatus; there was also a level of technological know-how varying widely from, but about on a par in local effectiveness with, that of Britain. In both nations, there could be no question that on the frontiers of industrial change rapid advances would continue.

3
The Patterns of Trade

Ocean trade made mercantile fortunes such as Stephen Girard's and supplied seaport traders with capital that could be invested in internal development. All the major American cities of 1790 owed their existence to the advantages of their harbors. Yet unlike industrial technology or domestic business, overseas trade was not to be a continuous stimulant on the frontiers of change. For both political and economic reasons not connected with industrial progress, foreign trade either grew or stagnated over lengthy periods. From 1773 to 1790 politics led to interruptions and diminished volume; from 1793 through 1807 foreign wars stimulated shipping as never before; but from 1808 to the mid-1820s external problems again checked the growth of international trade. The port cities had always grown from trade with their nearby hinterlands, and as backcountry population increased and methods of manufacture improved, intraregional trade became increasingly important. The size of these trade areas depended on the organization and finance of improvements in roads, rivers, and canals.

But business is an interwoven network, each strand of which affects the others, and underlying all the relations were, of course, the traits of American culture. The cultural characteristic of impatience with time- or labor-consuming ways of doing things, supported by a prevailing optimism, bred continual efforts at improvement in transportation and communication. Borrowing a term loan from a bank to finance inventories, for example, made merchants more conscious of the connection between time and the cost of working capital and therefore more anxious to speed up every process from original manufacture to customer remittance. The obvious solutions in each case were faster transportation and more efficient business transactions. Specialized firms in banking, insurance, and forwarding made these processes faster and more reliable, while fast sailing ships on frequent schedules and better roads, stage lines, and mail service substantially reduced the time between sending an order and receiving the goods.

In all these economies in time and efficiency no major advance in physical technology was involved. Yet the economist who has devoted the most recent attention to per capita income in the United States in this period, Paul A. David, finds a strong upsurge before 1808, when foreign trade was interrupted by the Embargo Act and subsequent regulations.[1] This surge in income calls attention to the relatively small size of the total manufacturing sector that gained from the new efficiency in the fabrication of metals, paper, wood, and textiles during this early period. Even though these mills were on what was ultimately the most important frontier of change, both the fixed capital in their machines and the value of their products were relatively small.[2]

I

A clear estimate of how much young, imaginative, and vigorous American entrepreneurship, inspired by newly won independence, was a factor in raising the efficiency of the world of business is not possible, for there are powerful forces operating outside of the business system, or what economists would call exogenous factors that cannot be part of any universal model or theory. Four such outside forces were helpful central government under the Constitution, a creative financial policy guided by Secretary of the Treasury Hamilton, wars in Europe, and reduction of barriers to interstate trade. The Constitution guaranteed the validity of business contracts throughout the nation and gave Congress the power to impose tariffs and grant subsidies, bounties, and loans to promote enterprise. The fishing industry, an essential source of income for New England, was granted subsidies; tariff duties for revenue were enacted; port charges favoring American ships were imposed; and some loans were made to canal companies and factories.

During the first Congress, Secretary of the Treasury Hamilton won laws to refund the national- and state-bonded indebtedness, incurred for the carrying on of the Revolution, at face value with new federal 6-percent bonds that should sell at about par. During the depressed years of the Confederation all government securities had fallen to a few cents on the dollar and had gradually drifted into the hands of merchants. When Hamilton's policy became clear, leading speculators like Robert Morris sent men on horseback into the more prosperous parts of the back-country to round up any bonds that might still be held by farmers or planters. In any case, merchants had been the principal holders of bonds, and, as a result, the passage of the funding and assumption acts put some $50 million in salable bonds in the hands of active business-men.

Another great supply of capital for economic development came as a result of wars in Europe that made the United States the chief neutral commerce carrier and forced Britain to relax the trade restrictions insti-tuted against the United States after the Revolution. Seizures of enemy vessels at sea by British and French privateers led to soaring shipping rates, which Americans operating with relative security could collect for routine voyages.

As trade volume increased, reexports to Europe from all of the West Indies and other belligerent ports grew rapidly. This increased volume of trade benefited New York more than the other northeastern ports. New York's harbor was incomparably better than that of any of its rivals and was served by three protected waterways—Long Island Sound and the Hudson and Raritan rivers. The more trade depended on economies from cutting the turnaround time of landing and loading goods for reex-port, the more New York profited. The city's merchants also had strong ties with British exporters and importers. Boston had a good harbor, but mileage and winds made it harder for small boats from the West Indies to reach than New York, and the volume of local goods was much smaller. Oscar and Mary Handlin do not think that the boom from 1793 through 1807 made up for the trade that had been lost to Mas-sachusetts by the Revolution.[3] While Baltimore and Philadelphia en-joyed commercial prosperity, both suffered from their long approaches through inland waterways, and Baltimore from interruptions in a large trade with continental Europe.[4]

As a result, Philadelphia, the great port of the late colonial and early national periods, lost its primacy in value of exports to New York by 1797, with the latter's margin of superiority depending on reexports. This shift from Philadelphia to New York illustrates a circularity of cause and effect involving population and trade. Other things being equal, the best market for cargo is in the biggest and richest city. Possessing these advantages gave Philadelphia its earlier supremacy. But as the war-inspired boom in the carrying and reexport trades went on, New York City, with its superior harbor and better transportation from its hinterland, gained the advantage. For the decade 1790–1800 it grew at the rate of 83 percent as compared to 45 percent for its rival. Consequently, by the turn of the century New York offered the best port as well as access to inland markets approximately as big as those of Philadelphia.

Faster turnover of goods and better communication were important factors in the snowballing of business volume in the port of New York. For example, based on the total number of trips per year, by 1820 boats for Charleston, South Carolina, left Philadelphia on the average of every ten days, whereas departures from New York averaged twice a week. Therefore an order would normally be delayed five days getting out of Philadelphia, as against less than two days from New York.[5] The port-to-port sailing time was about the same southward, but prevailing adverse winds on the Delaware Bay and Delaware River made the return trip swifter to New York. Thus less frequent ship departures and the hazards of winds and winter ice in the Delaware River cost Philadelphia practically all the cotton trade except for bales sold locally.

Meanwhile the China trade was opened by a joint New York–Philadelphia venture that dispatched the *Empress of China* in 1784. But up to early 1808, when the Embargo Act closed United States ports to imports and exports, the main stimulation to capital investment arising from trade came not from new markets but from freight charges and reexports.

The West India trade revived to its pre-Revolutionary level, but the needs of the islands failed to grow. Consequently the Caribbean trade, in which Philadelphia had been most active, became relatively less important to an expanding American economy. Similarly, the world market for Pennsylvania exports of lumber and flour remained nearly stationary. The only export with much promise of growth was cotton, which by 1807 accounted for about 30 percent of the value of United States domestic exports.[6] Many of the cotton bales were shipped directly to Liverpool from Charleston, Savannah, Mobile, or New Orleans; return cargoes from England generally came to New York, which offered the best market for supplying the South. Hence the southerners received payment for their cotton, rice, tobacco, and sugar indirectly in goods on coastwise ships chiefly from New York and to a lesser extent from Boston, which participated in the same trade cycle.

In 1807 President Jefferson decided to bring pressure on Britain to end frequent violations of the neutrality of American ships by joining Napoleon in a ban on all British imports. Since American trade was chiefly with England, Jefferson thought that to be effective the measure must stop all foreign trade. This economically "exogenous" measure, plus continuing self-imposed trade restrictions from 1809 to 1812 and then war against Britain until the end of 1814, had important effects on the short-run directions of American economic development.

Merchants no longer having use for their working capital in overseas trade turned to domestic investments, chiefly in building construction and inland transportation. The trade restrictions also provided domestic production the benefits of a protective tariff on iron and other metal products, glass, textiles, and some other less important imports. Industrial and urban growth were also stimulated by inflationary expansions of bank currency from 1811 to 1816 that made lonas and mortgages easier to carry. With the return of peace, normal competition with England, together with a decline in the domestic money supply from 1816 to 1819, caused difficulties in marketing for American manufacturing establishments, and many of those organized in the previous decade failed. Thus the long-run importance of the stimulation to mechanized production provided by the embargo and war years is hard to estimate, and there are no reliable statistics. Yet there was a considerable increase in the number of men with manufacturing experience.

A tariff bill put through Congress in 1816 with help from all sections raised duties somewhat, but, in general, not enough to overcome postwar British dumping and seaport merchants' preference for imports. Sales of large cargoes of British goods helped to developed the public auction system, particularly in New York, which was both the best market for such sales and the city with the most favorable regulatory laws. Sales by public auctions in turn contributed to the increasing dominance of the city as an import center. By 1821, 37 percent of all imports to the United States came through the port of New York, whereas only a fifth of the exports left from there.[7] In 1825 the ports of Baltimore, Boston, New York, and Philadelphia together handled 80 percent of United States imports but only 55 percent of the exports, the disparity being to a considerable extent the result of direct cotton shipments from southern ports to England, while southern purchases were made through the northern ports.

In 1819 a group of Quaker merchants in New York City started a trans-Atlantic packet line, the ships sailing monthly regardless of wind or weather is a striking example of the saving in time achieved by specialization and better utilization of facilities. A ship used mainly by a single merchant or partnership would only sail when a proper cargo for the voyage had been collected, which might take many weeks. Meanwhile capital overhead on ship and cargo went on inexorably adding to the cost. In contrast, a scheduled shipping line had a sailing date, and varying quantities of goods could be delivered only a few days before departure. Put another way, on the proprietary ship the last part of the cargo to arrive delayed the whole shipment, while on the liner or even on the tramp ship with frequent but unscheduled service goods could be dispatched more nearly when ready.

It is interesting that while the practice of scheduled sailings was an old one, it was first applied to the trans-Atlantic trade from the American end by the New York Quakers' Black Ball Line. Three years later Thomas P. Cope and other local merchants established a scheduled monthly line from Philadelphia to Liverpool. These packet boats, designed for speed and to carry more tonnage in relation to the size of the crew, not only facilitated more rapid turnover of imports and exports but also made the voyage less tedious for trans-Atlantic passengers. While the initiation of scheduled sailings had no direct connection with industrial growth, it illustrates the innovative thought and action that Americans were applying to all processes.

In the colonial period export and reexport trades had been of primary importance in building the port cities, from 1790 to 1825 the per capita contribution of foreign trade to the national income fell for several reasons: interior production and internal trade were rising rapidly, thus decreasing the share of the national income attributable to foreign trade; the failure of the West India trade to grow made this sector of the foreign trade relatively less important; and demand for American exports other than cotton failed to keep pace with growing national economies, here or abroad. On the basis of 100 for 1790, per capita foreign trade in 1800 was 55 (partly because of the undeclared war with France, 1798–1800), 45 in 1820, and only 30 in 1825.[8] The latter date, to be sure, represented a depressed year in cotton sales, which picked up rapidly thereafter, but the trend is obvious. In addition the terms of trade—

the relative price levels of exports and imports—were moving in a direction adverse to the United States. The inescapable conclusion from these figures is that while foreign trade was an initial stimulant in the late eighteenth century, it was not the chief basis for continuing economic growth. By 1815 the northeastern ports can be seen as growing centers for trade with their expanding hinterlands and for coastwise exports to the South. These local or regional interchanges became increasingly important in relation to those of foreign trade. On balance, the Northeast was a region prospering on a self-sufficient basis. Commenting on Douglas C. North's emphasis on the leading role of cotton exports, Stanley L. Engerman says that "the preconditions of growth were there, and external demand affected the pattern more than it did the existence of a rate of growth. . . . It is likely that growth is a rather pervasive process once certain conditions are met, and that clearly any one sector is only a small part of the economy."[9]

II

The trade of key importance was that spreading out from the large northeastern cities, which were also joined to each other by cheap transport and relatively fast communication.[10] To a considerable extent early industrialization in the United States is directly tied to the growth of cities and their nearby farming hinterlands. While immigrants were important in the early growth of the Middle States port cities, it may well be that had there been no foreign trade in the early Republic the interior interchange between hinterland and port city would still have led to industrialization at a more rapid rate than in contemporary continental Europe.

Major economic change in the late eighteenth and early nineteenth centuries in both Britain and the United States came from the speeding and cheapening of internal trade. While a responsive culture and a developed business system were prerequisites, and mill machinery and steampower were ultimately to be more important to later progress, the immediate developments on the frontiers of change were rather simple and old technologies applied on an unprecedented scale to transportation. In both needs and available resources the two nations presented important contrasts in geography, resources, and the pattern of population, as well as the dominant political contrast inherent in American colonial status until the Revolution. The latter discouraged any possible response by colonial legislatures or entrepreneurs to the interest in canals that quickened in Britain about 1760.

Britain was coming to be increasingly dependent on coal for fuel, and, except for a few seacoast mines, its economical distribution required canals. In addition, populous inland cities and the concentration of markets in London encouraged the construction and improvement of inland waterways. The United States offered sharp contrasts in all these respects. Wood was everywhere so plentiful that fuel, even for plants in large cities, was supplied from nearby forests. The major concentrations of population were all on the seacoast, on bays or navigable rivers. Trade was chiefly local rather than directed to one central metropolis.

The great British canal boom from 1785 to 1810, had some repercussions, however, in the United States. In 1793 William Weston, an English canal "engineer," came to Philadelphia to give advice on a projected Schuylkill-Susquehanna canal, and when the canal company failed to raise the necessary capital he stayed on until 1801 and advised on a number of other projects, including the Middlesex Canal in Massachusetts, finally completed in 1805. The problems of this canal illustrate the impatience of American builders who would not take sufficient pains to make sure that ditches were level and thickly enough "puddled" with clay to prevent leakage. Some of these flaws contributed to the Middlesex Canal's lack of success, but, in a broader view, population and intercity trade had not yet grown to a point where canals parallel to open water transport could pay off.[11] Only from 1820 on, when a growing interior population became an important supplier of cheap food to the eastern cities, did the United States require more efficient connections and experience a sustained boom in canal building.

Both nations needed hard-surfaced roads, but once again interior cities, more inland commerce, and the necessity of transporting coal led to a greater demand for such improvements in Britain. In response to rising demand, turnpike trusts were chartered that allowed for collection of tolls. Strongly resisted by local users, English toll roads nevertheless paid a profit and became more and more numerous throughout the last half of the eighteenth and beginning of the nineteenth centuries. Meanwhile, practical British "engineers" such as John Metcalfe, John MacAdam, and Thomas Telford developed "hard"-surfaced roads that were built on a bed of large stones filled in with crushed rock and topped off by gravel. MacAdam contributed the idea of building the rock structure above ground level to provide drainage, and Telford also won fame as a bridge designer.[12]

As with canals, America's needs for hard-surfaced roads, were less pressing than Britain's, and colonial status discouraged both early investment and legislative action. Before the Revolution highways were merely tracks, about fifty feet wide, cleared of stumps and rocks. Lacking any surfacing, they were impassable for heavy wagons during rainy periods. The best time of the year for shipment of goods was winter, when horses could pull greater weights twice as fast on sleds, but snow could be counted on only north of middle Pennsylvania and New Jersey. With the growth of the port cities after 1790, the introduction of new road-surfacing techniques, an ample supply of stone for building, and the capital generated by the profits of neutral trade, the United States took off on a long road building boom.

As might be expected, Pennsylvania, with its large volume of overland trucking in food products, wood, and iron, took the lead. When the Philadelphia and Lancaster Turnpike Company offered its shares in 1791, the stock was oversubscribed fourfold. The most prominent citizens were leading promoters, and William Bingham, who became more and more closely associated with Baring Brothers in London, was the president. Under Bingham's guidance the company in 1794 completed the first long intercity hard-surfaced road; it ran sixty miles. Temporarily earning satisfactory returns, it fed the boom in turnpike building. Between 1797 and 1807 Massachusetts chartered over fifty turnpike and bridge companies, and New York created eighty-eight, which together built nine hundred miles of road.[13] Meanwhile, Britain was averaging fifty-five new companies a year.[14] As more mileage—some of it competing and some to smaller towns—was completed, turnpike companies became less and less profitable, but the pace of building remained high because cities and sizable towns feared decline and extinction if they were not connected with the outside world by a hard-surfaced road even though the probable net earnings from tolls did not justify the expense. The peak of construction came in the mid-1820s, by which time only new communities still lacked roads and the bulk of state aid was going to trunkline canals. At the height of road building, New York, where construction had been the most extensive, had chartered over three hundred turnpike companies that built some five thousand miles of hard-surfaced road.[15] To meet the political demands of inland areas, Pennsylvania ultimately subscribed $2.3 million in state funds to turnpikes even though they seldom paid any steady return on their stock. State investments were most likely made without specific formation of state policies or attempts to influence turnpike management.[16]

While investments in bridge companies and urban financial enterprises could generally earn money for the state because their operation was relatively simple and expenses could be controlled, both long turnpikes, and later on canals, suffered from heavy maintenance costs and poor management. It was hard to enforce honesty on distant toll collectors, hard to avoid being robbed by local contractors, and, in America particularly, hard to get competent managers to devote themselves to an unprofitable enterprise. But the absence of dividends to stockholders should not obscure the large economic return to rural and urban producers and consumers from such "social-overhead capital." The benefits of communication and transportation accrued to the community in innumerable ways that could not be tapped at tollgates.

All high-cost inland transportation in the United States shared this problem of providing social benefits that could not be turned into profits for the company. Rather it was the owners of strategic properties, bridges, and necessary adjuncts or supplies that made large gains. Other than land or bridge owners, the most direct profit makers from turnpikes were tavern keepers and stagecoach proprietors, often one in the same. The Eastern Stage Coach Company of Boston, for example, was both large and prosperous, while the turnpikes it traveled showed a loss. By 1815 there was an average of one tavern every mile on the turnpike from Albany to Cherry Valley near Otsego Lake. In the 1790s three tavern keepers illustrated a growing type of enterprise by running "Genteel Stage Wagons" from New York City to Albany in two days at a $4.50 fare.[17] Fast stages ran twice daily between New York and Philadelphia, using relays of horses to make the trip without stopping overnight.

As with turnpikes, river steamboats were generally profitable only in the beginning. With merely six boats on northeastern rivers by 1811, the early ones made money. In fact, Livingston and Robert Fulton maintained a profitable state-granted monopoly of the waters of New York State until 1824, when the United States Supreme Court set aside the law in *Gibbons v. Ogden*. John Stevens of Hoboken, New Jersey, also made money from a Pennsylvania monopoly of steamboats between Burlington, Camden, Philadelphia, and New Castle on the Delaware. But by 1820 even the Ohio River trade was becoming overcrowded, and the courts of the newer states refused to allow agreements for price fixing and limitation of service on the grounds that such contracts were common law conspiracies in restraint of trade. Meanwhile, after 1824 the shipping and traveling public often benefited from rates that paid an overall profit only to the shipbuilders who franchised captains by selling them a share of the boat.[18]

It should be remembered that the great boon to economic growth from cheap river transportation was largely confined to America. Neither England nor other European countries had the counterparts of the Northeast Coast's pattern of big cities connected wholly or in part by rivers, sounds, or bays, often navigable for 150 miles or more inland, or of the great Ohio-Mississippi system that opened the entire middle of the continent to steamboats. Such widespread demand meant that before 1830 the chief importance of the steam engine in the United States was in powering boats.

III

Turnpikes and steamboats brought a new world of faster communication to the Middle States and areas of southern New England. In the mid 1790s there were five mails a week in both directions of the day trip from New York to Philadelphia. From New York to Boston a weekly mail took four or more days. Since mail traveled in passenger coaches, overnight stops significantly extended travel time for trips of more than one day. By 1810 travel from New York to Philadelphia and on to Baltimore took only a day between each city, while travel from New York to Boston still required overnight stops. Steamboats up Long Island Sound to Fall River, Massachusetts, from which Boston could be reached by stage, soon facilitated this trip.[19]

The immediate payoff of better intercity communication was much less than its long-run potential. As time went on, direct metropolitan area exchanges in goods, money, and information became more and more important, but until the mid-1830s such interchange was small compared with local trade for Philadelphia or local and ocean trade for Boston and New York. The completion of interior waterways, eliminating the necessity of transshipment between Providence and Norfolk in 1838, was more important to interregional trade than the improvement of turnpikes.

With postage rates averaging about a penny for six or seven miles, newspapers and business correspondence necessarily made up most of the mail between the major cities. When the *Pennsylvania Packet and Daily Advertiser* initiated daily newspaper publication in 1784, ten of its sixteen columns were advertising. Since neither this pioneer nor its imitators had more than a few hundred subscribers, profits depended chiefly on selling space. By 1800 there were twenty-four East Coast dailies, and some of the more business-oriented ones sold nine-tenths of their space to advertisers. Printing and publishing had become a major industry, as had papermaking. News traveled by exchanges between the papers, and inevitably New York as the port most readily reached became the news center, particularly for worldwide information.[20] More even than in the case of passengers, faster transmission of all types of commercial information was achieved through eliminating overnight stops. In 1835, 95 percent of the mail route mileage was still covered by stage or horseback, but mail now could go from New York to Baltimore in a day. Inevitably this quicker interchange of current knowledge increased intercity trade and led to better informed entrepreneurs.

Yet, the seminal forces for change were not only newspapers, roads, canals, faster and cheaper sailing ships, steamboats, or financial instruments. All these had existed for decades. Rather the old order was being inevitably ended by hammers, drills, and lathes in small metalworking shops that produced everything from hay rakes to steam engines. The change to new occupations was facilitated by increasingly efficient farms that fed the workers in the rapidly growing cities.

4
New Methods of Production, 1785—1825

Traditional literature about the industrial revolution emphasizes the transfer of technology from Europe, particularly from Britain, to the United States, but says little of the reverse flows, perhaps because they were often resisted. In addition, some historians have failed to describe the indigenous development of an industrial technology in America suited to the potential demands and resources of the local culture and geography.[1] Seminal innovations that led irrevocably to industrialization have been overlooked in traditional approaches that ask how big the particular machine, how widespread its use. These are not the crucial questions; what is crucial is the establishment of the processes for building that machine on a profitable, ongoing basis, the self-reinforcing process of machines building machines. Once a large urbanized area such as the lower Delaware Valley had highly mechanized flour mills and machine shops turning out metal products of many types, including high-pressure steam engines, it was not going to revert to a premachine stage. That it took some half a century for the initially small United States to rival Britain in total value of manufactured products measures results and tells nothing of causes, origins, and early growth, which are the major interest of this book.

I

By the late eighteenth century there was a Western world knowledge of machines and metals, written to some extent in learned papers but more usually transferred by itinerant master mechanics or imaginative entrepreneurs who had the help of skilled workers. What developed in the various nations, therefore, was the result of a complex of cultural interests and abilities responding to market demands on the basis of knowledge, resources, and geography. Consequently, the notion of "technological diffusion" is a very indefinite concept. In the United States Oliver Evan's flour mill in Delaware seems imaginatively indigenous; John Fitch's steamboats were somewhat influenced by an itinerant British mechanic; Samuel Slater's spinning mills were a transfer of British technology; while Jacob Perkins's nail-cutting machinery was an American advance that had a slow transition to Britain. [2]

An important sociocultural element in such easy interchange of technology is "the presence of appropriately skilled men and women," who make such choices intelligently. [3] A student of comparative Anglo-American textile technology, David John Jeremy, writes, "It is often overlooked that all the new machines preserved the core elements of many old devices, so . . . offered few learning difficulties to American workers. . . . American carpenters, cabinet makers, wheelwrights, ironmasters, blacksmiths, wire drawers, and clock makers (for brass gear cutting) could equal most of their British counterparts." Craftsmen in both nations, however, had difficulties in mastering some new interrelationships of components. [4]

A difference between Britain and the United States in the late eighteenth and early nineteenth centuries was that, because of rapid growth in America, building construction was always the chief form of capital investment and the chief occupation of skilled craftsmen. Without much exaggeration, investment in fixed capital for manufacturing equipment before 1825 may be seen as a spin-off from profits made in trade, real estate, and building. And, while the financing of building construction became easier, there was little progress in its technology during this period except for Perkins's invention of factory cut nails and the greater use of power sawing, so that building continued to be a large consumer of capital.

Another difference between industrialization in America and in Britain that was to last far into the nineteenth century had to do with wood and iron. Wood for fuel was becoming scarcer and scarcer in Britain; without coal for coke as a substitute for charcoal from wood, iron processing would have had to decline. In contrast, in early America wood was abundant everywhere, needing only to be cut. The result was not only the use of wood for fuel, but a wood-based technology that initially applied to mills, clock mechanisms, gears, and other types of machinery—including steam boilers. By the time of the Revolution, Americans had, as Robert P. Multhauf has put it, "managed to base on wood a civilization which seems in many ways superior—at least in retrospect—to that which succeeded it." [5]

It used to be widely believed that the unprecedentedly rapid adoption by American entrepreneurs of machine production after 1790 was owing to the fact that wages were much higher in America than in Britain, particularly for unskilled labor. This hypothesis has been extensively analyzed by Donald R. Adams, Jr. for the period 1790 to 1830, and his conclusion is, "My evidence clearly indicates that the advantages pursuant to the adoption of capital-intensive [i.e., labor-saving] techniques were greater in England." [6] Although there may be quibbles over exact amounts, from the standpoint of our broad overall view Adams's conclusion makes cultural or geographic causes seem clearly more important than incentives from "marginal costs" concerned with wages in explaining the differences between mechanization in Britain and the United States in the early nineteenth century.

By the middle of the eighteenth century Britain had improved productivity by the minute divisions of labor. In America at this time, as well as later, the mobility of labor from job to job and area to area, as well as a smaller market for any given product, checked this type of extreme specialization. When mechanization began to be rapid, the smaller size of American plants also facilitated changes in machinery, as did cultural attitudes that did not restrain scrapping and discard, practices which were encouraged, in fact, by the migratory character of both entrepreneurs and workers. [7] It is interesting that Peter Mathias sees the "trigger mechanisms" leading to rapid industrialization in Britain as rising demands, high wages, and scarce skilled labor, all of which were shared with the rapidly growing United States. [8]

Improvements in industrial methods in America had been to some degree held back by British colonial restrictions on manufacturing and the fact that provincial governments doubted their authority to create corporations for internal improvements. But the British prohibitions in 1734 and 1750 of some types of finished manufacture, including iron and steel, did not apply to existing plants, so that two steel and iron works continued in Pennsylvania.

The successful transitions to modern industrialization have generally been associated with the processing of supplies of raw materials, especially iron, and such was obviously the case in Britain and the United States. But, in part, American raw materials were different from those of the British Isles. While Pennsylvania iron and coal were essential to the great upsurge from the early 1840s on, in the period before 1825 wheat, timber, leather, and cotton were at least equally as important as iron. Each mill in a metropolitan area employed workers whose demands for other products had to be satisfied, and this "feedback" produced new shops to satisfy the growing market. The cheapness of food in America also meant more purchasing power for other commodities than in Britain or Europe. In addition, simplicity or lack of roundabout and complex processes of manufacture was an advantage in these earliest stages of industrialization, as new demand could be met more quickly with less investment.[9]

Although H. J. Habakkuk sees industrialization in the long run as growing from cheap iron and coal, he emphasizes the importance of transportation in Britain around the turn of the century.[10] Transportation was an essential component of industrialization in the United States, too. In early nineteenth-century America the machine spinning mill was of minor importance compared to the hard-surfaced road; the early steam engine was more significant for improvements in river transport than in manufacturing; and iron puddling and rolling were far less vital to immediate progress than canals.

After the Revolution, American enthusiasm for mechanical innovation that would increase domestic production appears to have been more widespread than historians have generally understood. Part of the misunderstanding comes from Alexander Hamilton's elaborate and unnecessary arguments against physiocrats or other imagined agrarian opponents in his Report on Manufactures.[11] Jefferson has been wrongly pictured as the leader of this opposition. To the point is Charles V. Hagnar's comment that in the 1790s "Thomas Jefferson, . . . a personal friend of my father, . . . indoctrinated him with the manufacturing fever. He started a cotton mill about the same time as the Nicholson venture."[12] Among the generation young in 1800, there was a growing belief that machines would soon produce a society of plenty.

II

Accelerating the pace of practical advance on the frontier of early technological change was the presence of many skilled artisan-entrepreneurs trying to improve processes, a group that existed in Britain and America alike. These inspired mechanics performed as artists. Their thinking was largely visual, or, put in terms of modern theories of the brain, they conceived devices as nonverbalized patterns in the right cranial hemisphere and then checked their practicality by reference to the calculating left lobe. Often no such process was necessary, the imagined improvement being obviously workable. Seen this way, Evans, Fitch, Fulton, Rumsey, Stevens, Whitney, and many others were artists in creating a new world of useful machines. Such men were inspired in Europe as well, but the creations of each nation bore the stamp of the local culture and physical environment.

In early industrialization what may be called the workbench skills and imagination were more important than scientific knowledge or the kinds of intellectual skills required in the twentieth century. It was said that practical, all-purpose machine builders were cheaper to hire in the United States than in Britain, presumably because there were more artisans with a wide variety of skills. In Britain, by contrast, the extreme division of labor in specialized shops had limited the range of individual skills.[13]

The high general competence of American workers led Benjamin Franklin to remark, "I do not know a single imported article into the northern colonies, but what they can either do without or make themselves."[14] Under threat of suspended trade with Britain, cloth factories using spinning jennies appeared in Philadelphia in 1775. By moving out of town during the British occupation (1777–78), Samuel Wetherill kept the textile business going and also became a pioneer dyer.[15]

The activities of American artisan-entrepreneurs from the 1780s on— James Rumsey's and Henry Voight's design for a water tube boiler, Evans's innovation in setting up a completely automated flour mill, Jacob Perkins's machine-made nails, Eli Whitney's world-influencing perfection of the cotton gin—were so spectacular that one needs continually to be reminded that the most important immediate spurs to development were in business incorporation, specialization, and transportation. Pushing against the frontiers of traditional practice were scores of impatient American artisans. Although some aspects of the environment tempted the less ambitious to hunt and fish, part of the population was probably the most industrious and future oriented of any in the world. "It was not the pace of work in America," writes Daniel T. Rodgers, "so much as its universality, its bewilderingly exalted status, the force of the idea itself."[16] Because of continual expansion and migration, the practical education of most boys, either rural or urban, was in learning to use tools, and a desire to share in the inevitable progress of the nation made the more imaginative impatient with the tools at hand. While measurement seems impossible, it may well be that the attitudes and perceptions of skilled labor in America—the nation's possession of what economists would now call "human capital"—largely made up for some scarcity and inelasticity in the supply of workers. The business proprietor's desire to substitute machinery for labor was in large part dictated by the impatience of the knowledgeable artisan with working for somebody else. A lathe or drilling machine stayed put while a fine gunsmith might not. The employed skilled labor force, therefore, may be seen as unreliable in ways other than in abilities or in initial short supply. Not only was it drawn off at the top by entrepreneurial opportunities in rapidly growing areas and elsewhere by a traditional desire to farm, but reliability was also undermined by the irregular work habits among the less ambitious who took jobs only when they needed them.[17]

The unique character of skilled labor in America may also be responsible for the position of the tool maker or fabricator in the marketplace. In Europe and even in England manufacturers tried to make what the merchants demanded. In the United States the manufacturing proprietor listened to his toolmakers and gave the merchants what was best to produce, a situation economists have called a producer- rather than a consumer-oriented system of manufacture.

III

A rapid rise of specialized shops or factories before 1815 should not obscure the fact that the period was the end of a longer one that Europeans have labeled proto-industrialism, a period in which wholesale and retail trade were the leading sectors of the nonagricultural economy and more manufactured goods were produced in households, both rural and urban, than in specialized plants.[18] In European nations there was generally a long period when the products of rural factories, dependent on putting-out systems, competed with those of the artisan guilds in the cities. In America there were no guilds capable of controlling production or distribution; in fact, in most states after 1810 there were no laws making apprenticeship enforceable. Factories using machinery and waterpower could locate in or near cities and sell their products without restriction. Consequently household or handicraft industry on a putting-out basis, often with considerable division of labor, could grow up in American cities as well as in the countryside.

Certain industries supplying food, shelter, and clothing were present in every locality of two hundred or three hundred families, and had been for generations. Waterpower applied to turning wheels was old. A sawmill, a gristmill, and a brewery, and perhaps a distillery and a tannery, were local necessities. Wearing apparel was made in homes, with recourse to mills for fulling and carding. Before 1800 each house, it was said, averaged a spinning wheel for every adult female, and half the houses had a loom for weaving, usually done by men.[19] In addition to such local industry, itinerant shoe, hat, and candle makers, iron-workers, and other artisans moved from place to place satisfying local demands.

These local handicraft industries, more than foreign imports, provided the competition for early waterpowered mills or shops that sought to sell their products beyond their immediate markets. Obviously, both household and neighborhood production would maintain their profitability in relation to three factors: the efficiency of the division of labor, the transportation costs of large-scale mechanized competitors, and the special qualities of the largely handmade products. Goods made by a carefully organized putting-out operation, using the greatest practical division of labor, were not necessarily confined to a local market. Interregional trade between Philadelphia and Boston, for example, was carried on in special varieties of homemade textiles.[20] Shoes made in the homes of Lynn, Massachusetts, and Roxboro, Pennsylvania, were sent up and down the coast. In fact, the ability of metropolitan plants to undersell the products of household industries in their own neighborhoods varied greatly with the type of product and the conditions of transportation. Well-organized household production of fine cloth could hold its own against coarser machine-made material, and did so in the Philadelphia area throughout this period. In the leading European centers handweaving of the finest materials continued into the late nineteenth century.

The slow pace of the mill's war of attrition against household manufacture is indicated in the census of 1810. In Pennsylvania, as a whole, household production of cloth was listed at $5.67 per capita, slightly above the national average, while in the counties along the Delaware River, where mill competition was keener, the average was $4.95. Similar variations were shown for New England counties. For the nation as a whole textile production was valued at $42 million, and household products made up 90 percent of that total. These statistics are, of course, highly unreliable, but no matter how high the degree of error in collecting and evaluating the information, the continuing predominance of household industry cannot be questioned.

An intermediate stage between the mechanized factory using waterpower and handwork done at home was the shop that brought together a large number of handworkers. Here there could be minute division of labor, hence a decreasing need for general skills, and constant supervision could ensure a more reliable volume of production. Such "factories" existed from the late colonial days in candlemaking and textiles. In 1782 Samuel Wetherill advertised several types of cloth from his "manufactury" in Philadelphia.[21] From the 1790s on, when the waterpowered Arkwright frame began to mechanize some American spinning, weavers were moved into factories to achieve balanced production.[22]

IV

If industrialization is seen as tools creating the demand for more tools, starting at the workbench and ending in the large factory, there are certain key metalworking industries involved at the core of the process. But if, in addition, the rate of progress is seen as associated with the entrepreneurship and levels of demand that come from a more productive agriculture and a lively business system developing products of the preindustrial age, then a wide range of only partially mechanized industries stimulate change in the system. The reverse of this mutual reinforcement may be seen in Third World nations, where a high-technology operation lacks a dynamic environment. While, as compared to industries employing steampower and metal machinery, such older industries as building construction, leather tanning, papermaking, printing, chemicals manufacture, glassmaking, ropemaking, shipbuilding, and textile manufacture may not individually seem to have led to general industrialization, clustered at large centers these industries produced increased demand and a highly favorable environment. In the United States all these activities could be found at the Northeast Coast port cities. Philadelphia was the main center of industry, while New York and Boston had relatively larger volumes of oceanic trade.

Of the mercantile wealth that accumulated, particularly from 1793 to

1808, most went into land or building construction. Even new manufacturing plants generally placed more money in land and buildings, including homes for workers, than in the machinery itself. The greatest technological advance of the turn of the century in construction work was the machine-made nail. Initially an American innovation credited to Jacob Perkins in 1796 and resisted by British builders for a generation, the mass produced nails were not only cheaper but easier to drive: they also tended to make wooden pegs obsolete except for decorative purposes.[23] At about the same time the screw augur was produced in the United States, but not used in England.[24]

In the early 1800s leather and lumber were as important as iron products. The two raw materials were closely connected. Hemlock trees had the best bark for tanning hides, and they were most abundant in New York and Pennsylvania. But tanning was a local industry carried on everywhere for local uses with whatever hides and barks were available, with Massachusetts, New York, and Pennsylvania having the chief plants selling leather for commercial uses.

From available records the transmission to America of tanning technology from the British Isles and France is not clear. In these nations between 1780 and 1800 there were important improvements. By adding lime water to the bark solution in which hides were soaked, David McBride of Dublin cut tanning time by one-third, or several months. Then Armand Seguin, an associate of Antoine Lavoisier in France, reduced soaking time to a matter of days by using dilute sulfuric acid. Yet, American experiments with these rather simple processes failed to show any great savings. A Delaware plant using the Seguin process after the War of 1812 did not experience a substantial reduction in costs.[25] One trouble may have been differences in the quality of hides, those tanned commercially in the Northeast Coast ports coming chiefly from Argentina and Spain. The tanning industry appears to have been highly competitive, and good management of plant and disposal of inventory may have been more important than savings from technology.

A boost for leather production occurred from an indigenous technological advance. Leather belting rather than gears had been used in Evans's early flour mills and in some other industries before 1800, but the general adoption of leather for power transmission came around 1825 with its use in large Massachusetts textile mills. The enormous gear wheels cost more to install, produced deafening noise, shook wooden buildings to pieces, and required expert machining. Drive by gear wheels continued, however, in Britain, where factories were generally constructed of brick or stone. The rest of Europe adopted leather belting.[26]

Cheap paper, which helped make possible the low-priced daily newspaper and ultimately a civilization deluged with communications on paper, surely represents one of the major advances of industrialization. The beginnings of change go back, at least, to 1780 and Nathan Sellers's improved straightening board, followed by various improvements in the use of waterpower.[27] By 1810 papermaking was carried on everywhere in the United States, but about one-third of the total activity was in the Philadelphia area. As early as 1787 there were half a dozen mills in New Castle County, Delaware, and by 1797, sixty mills on the Brandywine. Visiting the mills in 1788, Brissot de Warville observed, "Their process in making paper is much simpler than ours. [But] specimens equal . . . the finest made in France." Benjamin Franklin claimed he was instrumental in starting eighteen paper mills, and found American know-how equal to the discussions published in the transactions of the French Academy.[28] It is safe to say that no other nation had one of its three or four most distinguished citizens so interested in paper manufacture. But deliberate differences in quality and type of product make precise comparison with Europe difficult.

Papermaking also made an early start in New England, and by 1810 the biggest single mill was at Chicopee, Massachusetts. Nicholas L. Robert took out a United States patent on the Fourdrinier machine in 1799, but its small saving in labor did not attract capital and he sold the patent to an Englishman in 1804.[29] By 1816 John Ames of Springfield, Massachusetts, and Thomas Gilpin of Philadelphia had both "invented" cylindrical paper machines copied from an English model. They were more popular in the United States than the flat-bed Fourdrinier machine that had been perfected in Britain during the preceding decade. Not until 1828 did a Fourdrinier machine establish itself as a competitor to cylinder papermaking in the United States.

Philadelphia was the center of the early nineteenth-century printing industry, and the important advances first appeared there. By introducing iron presses around 1800, Adam Ramage put an end to imports.[30] Type foundries had appeared in America as early as the Revolution, but the first commercially successful plant manufacturing type from hand molds was built by Blaine, Binney, and Ronaldson in 1796. While their advance was nationally acclaimed as one of the most important in the history of the industry, it was not unique to the United States.[31] In 1816 George E. Clymer introduced distinctive improvements in the operation of printing presses.[32]

From the colonial period on the Philadelphia area was also the chemical center of the nation, and by the mid-nineteenth century the board of trade claimed that the city produced more pharmaceuticals than any other in the world. Philadelphia also dominated the national market for paints and dyes. In part a chemical process, glassmaking was distributed all along the Northeast Coast. Regardless of the size of the particular plant—one at New Bremen, Maryland, employed from four hundred to five hundred workers in 1790—glass remained a hand labor process requiring skills that were generally supplied by British or German immigrants.[33]

From colonial days on, the manufacture of rope and twine from hemp had been a major industry, only a part of whose product went into ship fitting. As with glass manufacture, there were rope walks up and down the Northeast Coast, and again like glass there was little advance in technology. By 1810 Philadelphia and Providence claimed the highest number of employees in rope and twine.

Shipbuilders, the chief customers for rope, were also widely distributed. Northern Massachusetts and Maine remained large producers, but since up to the time of iron steamships in the mid-1840s there were no significant economies from large-scale construction, shipbuilders could operate on small rivers such as those in southern New Jersey that would carry the completed boat to Delaware Bay. The largest clusters of shipyards were around Boston, New York, and on the Delaware River from the falls at Trenton to New Castle at the head of the bay, a concentration that has led David B. Tyler to call the Delaware River area the American Clyde.[34]

Shipbuilders occupied a unique position in the progress of industrialization from 1790 to 1850. Up to 1830 they did not innovate in the area of machine processes, but with the help of models by the Philadelphia architect and builder Joshua Humphreys, they developed new efficiencies in a basically stable design. In his Philadelphia yards Humphreys had built the ships for John Paul Jones's squadron in the Revolutionary War. The future of his yards was assured when the British scuttled all American ships in Philadelphia in 1778. As a result, by 1800 the port had three hundred newly designed merchant vessels and was selling these superior ships to foreign nations. The American frigates that defeated the Barbary pirates were designed by Humpreys. One of his merchant vessels, the *Rebecca Sims*, built in 1801, sailed from Delaware Bay to the Mersey River near Liverpool in fourteen days, a speed never equaled under sail. Basically, the Humphreys ships were broader and longer, had less superstructure, and carried more sail than earlier models.[35] Soon the major shipyards up and down the Northeast Coast were copying his designs.

V

Textile manufacture has often appeared to typify the maturing industrial revolution. Not only have early innovations in textile machinery seemed to spearhead industrialization, but textile plants generally brought together larger numbers of workers in factories than any other industries; after 1815 some plants employed four or five hundred people. But emphasis on numbers of employees and the problems of converting human beings from agricultural to factory lives can obscure the more basic technological importance of early mechanization in the processing of raw materials other than wool and cotton. In the United States it also obscures the significance of early steam engines and the rapid development of iron and its products. And, in fact, factory production of finished textiles came late in the development of American machine technology. Until the Embargo of 1807 cut off British competition, the few American mills powered by water were, as in England, limited to spinning. It was the protection given to native industries by interruptions in British trade from 1808 to 1815 that led to the first mechanization of cotton weaving in Massachusetts, Pennsylvania, and Rhode Island. Yet textile machinery did demonstrate some new possibilities of mechanization and ultimately stimulated the machine tool industry in cities such as Philadelphia and Providence.[36]

As in all American attempts at manufacturing, the business problem in textiles was to find the type of product that with good technology and the moderate protection provided by the tariff could survive both household and British competition. Because (except for carpets) textiles were lightweight in relation to their value, domestic operations were not nearly as well protected from British competition by the freight charges that burdened heavier products. In the early Republic the success of a mill industry in cotton textiles must have seemed uncertain, as the advantages over household production were small and British competition was intense. But the combination of merchants looking for investment of the high profits of 1790 through 1807 and the interruptions of British imports from 1808 on nourished an infant industry in cheap cottons that, with higher tariff protection in 1816, was able to survive normal foreign competition. In the coarser types of thread and cloth manufacture the only competition continuing after this date was from household production.

Textile manufacture in America has three quite distinct periods. In spite of rather easy access to British technological know-how, bad planning and bad luck prevented the success of mills for waterpowered cotton spinning before the early 1790s.[37] Although there were a few hand-operated factories, particularly in woolen carpetmaking in Philadelphia, production was normally carried on in rural and urban households. Fine cloth was imported from Europe. It is also a feature of the early period in cotton that warps, at least, were of linen thread.[38] A second period, 1790–1814, is marked by the development of American carding machinery and the introduction of waterpowered spinning with jennies, mules, or frames. Such mechanization moved a small part of the production of cotton thread from homes into factories. In the third period, 1814–25, weaving by power looms, adopted at about the same rate in Britain and the United States, completed mechanization of the basic processes of cotton textile manufacture.

Merchant capitalists wanting to invest in textile manufacture, particularly in New England, which after 1808 lacked other promising local opportunities, faced two initial problems: building efficient waterpowered jennies, mules, or frames for spinning, and finding supervisors who could boss mill workers and keep the machinery in repair.[39] Fires that destroyed mills and their wooden machinery were an additional, unpredictable trouble. They were so frequent in mills in the Delaware Valley that there was suspicion of arson either by handworkers or British agents. In any event, a cotton mill was highly flammable. All the earliest mills, from Maryland to Massachusetts, failed because of one or more of these difficulties.

Then in late 1789 Samuel Slater, an émigré British mechanic with supervisory experience, arrived in New York and took a job in a cotton factory that was relying on hand power. His original aim was to find Philadelphia capitalists who would finance a modern spinning mill, but there was less interest shown by men in this oldest and largest center of handmade cloth than in Rhode Island, where a wealthy merchant,

Moses Brown, wanted to promote waterpowered manufacturing. Working for Almy and Brown (Moses's son-in-law and cousin), Slater built a mill in Pawtucket and successfully produced thread by the end of 1790. Between then and 1815 the firm established a score of waterpowered carding and spinning mills in southern New England, usually by lending capital to local entrepreneurs and contracting to market the product. A similar development went on in the Middle States. The number of skilled workers the mills required was small. In both regions they were generally immigrants; in the Middle States some skilled laborers were also drawn from Philadelphia.[40]

Almy and Brown had a major problem in marketing, for they sought to sell cotton thread to retailers used to dealing in flax (linen) and wool. Their ultimate success in creating demand for cotton thread illustrates a general process in the development of technology. An improvement in one stage of production—in this case the "flying" shuttle for weaving—produces a disequilibrium at the next stage and the need for more technological improvement. By 1810, however, waterpowered spinning mills near or in Philadelphia, and at least one steampowered mill, were producing thread in quantities that even with flying shuttles could not be woven by hand.[41] One spinning mill in Baltimore, for example, operated eight thousand spindles in 1812.[42] When putting out the weaving failed to keep up with the thread coming to market, the next step was to bring weavers together in plants where they could be worked for longer hours. It was claimed that with good supervision these factory workers would turn out ten times as much as they would working off and on at home.

The power loom for weaving had a relatively long history that began with a commercially unsatisfactory model designed in England by Edmund Cartwright in 1787. Inventors in both America and Britain sought to make improvements, but the Americans lacked a good model on which to work. Improvements by William Horrocks of Stockport, England, from 1803 to 1813 made power looms competitive with handweaving for coarse cloth. In spite of patents issued for power looms in the United States, few manufacturers or distributors of cheap cloth were prepared to risk the large capital necessary to build and install an American design or to smuggle plans from Britain, for the goods would have to compete with both household and British cloth. A power loom installed at Taunton, Massachusetts, in 1812, did not attract imitation.

With the fairly complete halt of British cotton imports from the outbreak of hostilities in spring of 1812 until the beginning of 1815, at least three more groups of investors were led to attempt power weaving. A group in Lancaster, Pennsylvania, with only $128,000 in paid-in capital and presumably an American-designed power loom, started an operation for making a medium-coarse grade of cotton cloth at the very end of the war. No doubt well served by its location sixty miles from a seaport, it managed to survive British dumping of cloth on the American market in 1815 and 1816, but it could not weather the panic of 1819.[43] In addition to the pressure of British dumping, American textile mills also suffered from control of inland store credit by mercantile importers. Some country mills found they could not place their goods in nearby stores.

A mill financed by Boston merchants at Waltham, Massachusetts, with a slightly novel loom designed by Paul Moody from Francis Cabot Lowell's recollections and drawings of British machines, began production late in 1814. Lowell, a member of the most influential merchant aristocracy, went to Washington and won a minimum duty of 6.25 cents per yard in the tariff of 1816, a fee high enough to protect the cheap cloth of Waltham but apparently not the slightly better grade cloth of Lancaster; it should be remembered that most of the British cloth at this period was handwoven. In addition to power looms Waltham also had the advantage of plenty of capital. An elite group that came to be known as the Boston Associates, which included the wealthy merchant Nathan Appleton, became convinced of the profitability of the well-protected manufacture of cheap cloth. They made large and successful investments in mills on the Merrimack River at Lowell and, in the 1820s, in other areas as well. These mills, having the biggest sources of waterpower, remained the largest in the United States and attracted many foreign visitors.

Another early introduction of power weaving came through William Gilmore, who in 1815 brought knowledge of the so-called Scotch or crank loom, as opposed to Moody's cam-driven loom. Slater and his associates decided against power weaving, as had most English firms up to this time, but other mills in the Providence area contracted for a dozen of Gilmore's looms, which operated successfully.[44]

Thus by 1825 cotton textile manufacture had become completely mechanized, with the United States slightly, if at all, behind Britain in the widespread adoption of power weaving. In fact, in 1827 the *Leeds Mercury* credited America with introducing power looms for woolen weaving when there were none in Britain. In contrast to the heavy industry axis from Delaware to upstate New York, cheap cotton textile manufacture by machines was most concentrated along the numerous sources of waterpower from Connecticut to eastern Massachusetts, with Rhode Island as the center. Better-quality textile manufacture needing more skilled labor remained clustered from Pennsylvania to Maryland.

In spite of these developments, it is hard to equate mechanization in the textile industry with general industrialization. Since household manufacture used family labor that was otherwise partially unemployed, Victor S. Clark writes, "Though more yards of cloth were made in 1840 than in 1790, the increase was not as great as manufacturing records suggest. Converted into pounds of wool, cotton and flax used for each inhabitant, the increment would not be imposing."[45] Furthermore, in the language of economics, textiles lacked strong backward and forward linkages that through the operation of demand and supply would necessarily lead to further industrialization.[46]

VI

America's seminal achievements of the early period of industrialization were not in leather, paper, chemicals, glass, shipbuilding, textiles, or other industries that followed British practices. America's achievements were, instead, in the machine processing of raw materials, in river steamboats, and the making of the tools necessary for such operations. Each of the nations that has developed from processing its own raw materials has pursued a different path set by the qualities of the products and their markets. Sweden, for example, led the Western world in the quality of its pig iron for cutting tools not because Swedish artisans knew more about smelting but because they had purer ore. Similarly the United States led the world in the mechanization of flour production because it had the largest demand focused on areas of supply that fed only a few ports. In both cases the question of whether a nation would proceed to higher levels of industrialization or not was decided by its culture, specifically by the response of its artisan-entrepreneurs to the possibilities opened to them.

The American invention of the greatest immediate world importance during these years, and free from Old World influence, was Eli Whitney's cotton gin in 1793. A simple mechanism for separating cotton balls from their husks and seeds, it solved the chief labor problem in cotton production and made American cotton competitive in price with that of India, Egypt, or other subtropical producers operating where labor was cheap. Since the device was easy to imitate and Whitney a poor businessman, this invention that made possible the age of cheap cotton cloth never made the inventor rich. After 1800 Whitney was to gain fame as an arms manufacturer striving to fulfill federal and foreign government contracts for guns claimed to have interchangeable parts. While he, and others such as Simeon North, sought to achieve the widespread European goal of interchangeable parts, no one either in the United States, or earlier in France, produced parts that did not need filing in order to fit in a new gun. John Hall, born in New England, came much closer to achieving interchangeability in his manufacture of gun parts at Harpers Ferry Armory in Virginia (see chapter 5).

In America, with its population doubling every twenty years and adult males generally building new wooden homes, the demand for wood products was immense. But native resources and processors were able to meet that demand and more; cut lumber and furniture were exported to the West Indies. Sawmills were on every major stream, and in 1803 the application of steam to a sawmill in New York City marked the second use of such an engine in manufacturing.[47]

Americans were definitely the leaders in technological advances in woodworking. Since they had newer mills, Americans of the early nineteenth century probably used circular and band saws more than did Europeans.[48] Visitors to Britain saw no power saws in use there. H. J. Habakkuk goes so far as to say that all improvements in woodworking machinery from 1815 to 1851 were made in the United States.[49] Improvements in the woodworking industry illustrate the wasteful character of some American technology. In general they saved labor and time but used an extravagant amount of wood. Thicker, heavier, faster saws generated piles of sawdust that would have shocked a European millowner. A great deal of woodworking was done on farms and in households and so does not show up in the statistics; consequently wood products do not approach leather products in annual market value.

As in the preparation of cotton and wood for further use, large-scale demand prompted innovation in the processing of wheat. The chief United States export from the Middle States during the last half of the eighteenth and early part of the nineteenth centuries was flour. In a family-owned flour mill in Delaware, Oliver Evans, a young artisan, trained as a wagonmaker, began perfecting labor-saving improvements. In his widely varied mechanical interests Evans may serve as the archetype of the able American artisan. Brought up in an environment where surplus land and consequent migration kept labor scarce, his imagination, and that of many others, turned to how to do things with less human effort. While an economic basis for such speculation is obvious, the thought itself was not concerned with marginal costs or scarcity of particular types of workers. Rather imagining easier ways of doing things became a consuming interest in America. Eugene S. Ferguson calls this trait "America's . . . strong romantic and emotional . . . involvement with its technology."[50] Even where no new technology evolved, existing devices were used in labor-saving ways. Shop practices and processes were changed around to prevent wasted motion; machines were used more continuously.

But Evans proved to be far more than an ingenious mechanic; his automated flour mill, as Joseph Wickham Roe has claimed "practically initiated the 'modern science' of handling materials."[51] There was no mill like it anywhere. This concept of the modern factory without workers no doubt came to Evans in part as a result of the general American environmental pressure to save labor, but, in addition, he simply loved machines. Like other inventors, he did not start from scratch. Rather he took an already mechanized process requiring about three workers and carried existing methods to their logical conclusion—a mill with a single worker, a supervisor who saw the grain poured in at one side and flour discharged at the other. The long-term significance of this invention, perfected and patented by 1787, was not in producing very large profits for flour millers or in leading directly to new types of industrialization, but rather in initiating the idea of the automated factory, which became an ideal of American culture.

Up to the 1850s Evans's *Young Mill-wright and Miller's Guide* (1795) was in print and went through many editions. Soon Evans's mills were being installed by others in the Maryland-Delaware-Pennsylvania exporting area. Evans now felt sure that he could sell his patents in England. But there flour milling was small scale and local; hence the proprietors could not foresee profits from a capital investment that could only be repaid from a relatively high volume of production. In the United States, however, flour milling was to remain the principal industry in value of product until after the Civil War. Since in most other lines of production the automated factory was still only a vision—even in the late twentieth century—for this patent alone Evans should be regarded as one of the world's most important inventors.[52] An aspect of his mill machinery, the importance of which was overlooked at the time even by Evans himself, was the transmission of power by leather belting rather than gears.

Evans was a theorist as well as a practical, artistic innovator, and his interests included all types of machinery. In 1772, no doubt aware of James Watt's patent of 1769, Evans at age seventeen designed a better condensing steam engine, but he could not raise the capital needed for a working model. Meanwhile, although Watt in Scotland patented an improved, reciprocating engine in 1781, Evans continued to think of ways further to improve the efficiency of such engines. By 1785 both inventors had conceived of a high-pressure engine capable of delivering several times more horsepower for a given size and weight than the low-pressure type, but Watt regarded the boiler pressure as dangerous. Evans continued to experiment, and in 1801 he built a modern type of high-pressure steam engine. By this time Richard Trevithick and other British and French engineers had reached the same stage of advance, so that while world priority in construction of a commercially used high-pressure steam engine can be claimed for Evans, the whole development from 1770 on was going forward in America, Britain, and France and the priority of Evans is not as clear as in the case of the automated factory. But the first use of a high-pressure steam engine in manufacturing came in 1802, when his engine was installed in his Philadelphia plant making gypsum fertilizer. Evans proceeded to manufacture and sell high-pressure steam engines from 1803 until his death in 1819, including one for a steamboat in Austria, and his factory was continued by his heirs. Never a man to hide his light under a bushel, in 1805 Evans published a steam engineer's guide that predated any such work in Britain and included a plan for artificial refrigeration.[53]

By 1804 Evans was prepared to build steam trucks for use on the new turnpikes or on rails, and in 1809 he offered to invest all of his money in a railroad. But he was not rich, and he failed to interest merchant capitalists. Instead his shop filled orders for steam engines for slitting and rolling mills, sugar and cider mills, and steamboats, as well as making various iron products. Among his other inventions were a plan for gas lighting, a solar boiler, central heating, a refrigeration machine, a machine gun, an evaporator, a self-oiling shaft bearing, and a gear shift for his steam wagon.

Only for plants within cities and for navigation was early steampower efficient: elsewhere in the Northeast the many fast-flowing streams

made waterpower cheaper than either American or British
most important early American use of steam was in river
John Fitch of Philadelphia and James Rumsey of the Balumore
both conceived of the use of steam for boats about 1785. Being equally
impecunious they could do no building, but both received federal patents on the same day in 1791. By this time Rumsey had gone to England in search of capital, and he died there in 1792. Fitch, however,
had been able to put together a small company that from 1788 to 1791
financed and operated passenger boats on the Delaware River. Since the
ventures were not commercially successful he is generally not credited
with "inventing" the steamboat.

Three factors stand out in Fitch's failure. With some advice from an
English mechanic named John Hall, Fitch and Henry Voight, a clock-
maker, did practically all the designing; they did not have the help of
men familiar with the size relationships of low-pressure steam engines.
Consequently they made errors particularly in the size of cylinder necessary for fast upstream operation and also in reliable condensers. A second factor in Fitch's failure was the size of his steamboats; steamboats
gain in efficiency from increased size, and both of Fitch's boats were too
small. Finally there was the river on which Fitch's company operated.
The Delaware is wide, the current moderate, and navigation ends at
falls only about thirty miles upstream from Philadelphia. With Burlington, New Jersey, the only city upstream within reach, a slow steamboat
could not save enough time as against ferry and stage to compensate for
possible breakdowns. While Fitch's efforts ended with the destruction of
his boats in a storm and subsequent lack of capital, had the steamboats
promised greater profits more money could surely have been raised. As
it was, even if Fitch had been a suave, sober businessman, which he
was not, he probably could not have secured further support. [54]

The ultimate commercial triumph of ex-Pennsylvanian Robert Fulton in 1807 resulted from the reversal of the difficulties that had
harassed Fitch a generation earlier. Fulton, working in New York City,
had the backing of the very wealthy and politically powerful Robert Livingston. After a failure with the wrong type of boat, largely designed and
powered at Nicholas Roosevelt's Soho Plant in New Jersey, Fulton and
Livingston ordered engine designs and moving parts from Bolton and
Watt in England. But their success was due chiefly to their building a
big boat on a busy river navigable for nearly 150 miles inland. To ensure their market, Livingston won a twenty-year monopoly of steam

navigation of the waters of New York, and Fulton, a good businessman, went into manufacturing steamboats on the Jersey side of the river. Winning state monopolies of use became more important than being granted American patents, which were weak, and John Stevens and other mechanical entrepreneurs battled the Livingston-Fulton interests in state legislatures for many years. In general, Stevens won on the Delaware and Livingston and Fulton on the Hudson.[55]

The ultimate triumph of the steamboat as the major means of river travel depended, however, on the utilization of Evans's type of high-pressure engine. The low-pressure engines used by Rumsey, Fitch, and Fulton produced very little power for their size and weight; since relatively less horsepower per ton was needed as boat size increased, the increased size of Fulton's *Claremont* was one reason for its success. But when Nicholas Roosevelt went to New Orleans and built a boat to go up the Mississippi, the low-pressure engine proved inadequate regardless of size. Successful navigation depended on adoption of high pressure. Evans built a high-pressure steamboat for the Mississippi about 1803, but it was carried inland in Louisiana and was stranded in a spring flood; the engine was transferred to a sawmill. The ultimate conquest of the Mississippi system by steamboats came from the upper end. Evans's son started an engine works in Pittsburgh in 1811; and at Brownsville on the Monongahela, Daniel French began building a type of engine similar to Evans's but with a horizontal cylinder. A boat built by Henry Shreve and powered at Brownsville with a French engine steamed from New Orleans back upriver to Brownsville in 1815.[56] In all this conquest by steam of the mighty and fast-flowing American rivers, the influence of Europe is scarcely discernible. In 1811, when the United States had seven steamboats operating on eastern rivers, Britain had only one. Here again success came from the drives of American culture operating on a new frontier rather than from the diffusion of Old World technology.[57]

VII

Supporting America's achievements in the machine processing of raw materials and in river steamboats were developments in mining and metalworking that were to change machinery from wood to iron and create a machine tool industry. Mining of coal and iron—the two raw materials that were ultimately to become most important to Pennsylvania and the nation—expanded only gradually. In the early period soft coal came principally from Virginia and Nova Scotia. Even by 1825 Pennsylvania anthracite was only beginning to become the universal heating fuel throughout the Northeast. Everywhere there were still forests and cheap wood. Iron had a more varied early history. Until Henry Cort commercialized processing with coke in 1784, England lacked the necessary charcoal for large increases in finished ironmaking. Thus, in the colonial period America exported pig and bar iron, with Britain as the chief customer. Then within only a few years there was a switch; by 1790 Britain was a large exporter of iron, and the American product was confined to local uses.

Iron deposits in bogs and near the surface of the ground were found in every colony from Virginia on North. While Pennsylvania accounted for half of colonial iron, until sometime between the Revolution and the 1820s iron was mined and worked all along the Northeast Coast.[58] Only as this surface ore began to run out was there increasing reliance on the big and deep mines in Maryland, southeastern Pennsylvania, and near Lake Champlain in New York State.

Before the 1850s no one in the world understood the metallurgy of iron or steel. We now know that the ores of southeastern Pennsylvania were high in silicon and phosphorous and were best smelted with pure charcoal and plenty of lime. Early American ironmasters in this area have often been criticized for not using coke, for which eastern coal was unsuited, and for extravagant use of limestone. Actually they were doing the best they could by rule of thumb to produce wrought iron with the qualities demanded by their customers. Russian and Swedish pig was preferred for delicate machinery and sharp edges, but American iron would do for the much larger production in castings, bars, horseshoes, and myriad other local uses. In rapidly growing America the largest demand for iron was for stoves and implements for farm and household, much of which was supplied by local works from castings made at the same nearby furnace. This kind of iron was also used to strengthen boats. Compared to demands for cast iron, the domestic market for high quality wrought iron for tools, guns, and machinery was relatively small.

Conditions in the United States dictated still other differences from Britain in iron matellurgy. Abundant waterpower on the tributaries of the Delaware and other eastern rivers made it possible to purify pig iron through the hammering process, whereas in Britain, with its forced reliance on steam and greater availability of local labor, puddling and rolling were cheaper ways of shaping and purifying iron. In the first process the iron was heated to soften it and then pounded by waterpowered trip-hammers to expel cinders and other impurities left from the original smelting and reheating of the ore. After a long period of hammering the carbon content of the iron would drop to a point where it became almost as tough and malleable as steel. In the puddling and rolling process the iron was melted in pots, while workers stirred the mass, and finally turned out as soft balls of metal that could be made into sheet, beams, or rails by being passed many times through rollers. The resulting iron was not as satisfactory as hammered bar for tools and machine parts, but rolling mills produced superior sheet iron. Their advantage was soon recognized in the United States, but the dates of the first installations are uncertain. Josiah White, who in 1809 built a plant at Falls of the Schuylkill in Phildelphia County to manufacture nails, wire, and, later on, screws, is said to have had a rolling mill from the start. Certainly the Lukens firm of nearby Coatesville and other iron processors introduced rolling shortly after the War of 1812. One of the largest early plants was Mark Richards's rolling and nail mill at Manayunk on the Schuylkill; it was reported to employ over six hundred in 1828.[59] Practically nothing is known about the internal organization of these big ironworks.

So strong is the assumption in earlier writing of United States technological backwardness that American practices have never been considered as the best adaptations to local conditions. Pioneer advances in metallurgy, such as the annealing of brass and iron by Nathan Sellers of Philadelphia in the 1780s—a process that reached England only more than a decade later—are overlooked. When George Escol Sellers, the grandson of Nathan Sellers, went to Britain in 1832, he judged English ironworking shops to be rather backward in machinery for large-scale operations.[60]

In both Britain and the United States "sunk capital," of which there was much in Middle States iron manufacturing by the early nineteenth century, undoubtedly led to the retention of some archaic methods, but since Britain had been the leader in ironmaking, one suspects that more careful examination would reveal more holdovers from the past there than in the United States. The smaller size of American works in an industry where economies of scale were still not critical also allowed for easier change and experimentation. G. E. Sellers told a British iron manufacturer that "he must bear in mind that America's start in mechanical art was at the point England had reached without her prejudices."[61]

Usually it cannot be determined from historical records whether manufacturers were using the most efficient methods for their particular needs. Sellers and Pennock, known for their innovations, relied wholly on forged iron from nearby Coatesville for their Philadelphia plant employing two hundred men to make fire engines for world export.[62] One has to conclude that, since they could easily have shifted to imported iron, the local iron they used did their work more cheaply and effectively. Such arrangements were presumably more common after iron received additional tariff protection in 1818.

Whether imported or from domestic sources, iron was readily available in all the major manufacturing centers, and fuel for working it, chiefly wood in the early days, was abundant. It was not just a few brilliant mechanics such as Oliver Evans who were responsible for ushering in the iron age; rather it was brought in by the scores of machine shops working with metal that existed in or near to all the major cities, but in the early days chiefly in Philadelphia. Each such shop was a potential source of improvement in lathes, drills, and milling machinery or dozens of other advances in the processing of iron. For example, John Hall at Harpers Ferry Armory is said to have started about 1817 to remove excess iron from castings or other shapes by milling, a process only later adopted in Britain. Similarly, die forging may have first developed in the Colt shop in Connecticut.[63]

In Philadelphia by 1810 there were half a dozen ironworking shops within four blocks of each other that collectively constituted a machine tool industry, a basic requisite of industrial progress. It was this convergence of machine work in a few urban areas, rather than an occasional invention, that ensured the continuation of technological change.[64] Lacking such support from local enterprise, the "high technology" of a period will not take lasting root. That highly specialized British machinists were more skilled at their particular tasks than their counterparts in the United States was relatively unimportant. Skills in America were adequate for the advance of local industrial technology.

In the big cities of the Northeast there was continuous interchange of information, special equipment, routine subcontracting for parts or operations, and in-house manufacture of machines by goods producers. A finished steam engine might have parts from several shops.[65] The early New England textile mills near the shops of Providence and Bos-

ton were able to assemble their own machinery and later to supply it to
other mills. But specialization in the manufacture of textile machinery
came slowly; not until 1810 is there a reliable record of such shops at
Pawtucket, Rhode Island, and Holmesburg, near Philadelphia.[66] The
clustering of urban machine shops also led to a large supply of skilled
labor that could be relied on in replacements or new operations.

One of the best examples of the need for supportive shops and skilled
workers for high-technology operations is the dismal early history of the
Harpers Ferry Armory authorized by Congress in 1798. Placed for poli-
tico-business reasons on land belonging to the Potomac Company in
which George Washington had a large interest, it was far out in the
backcountry of Virginia. Local farming and townspeople were hostile to
skilled workers from Philadelphia, hence many of the latter would not
stay. For more than a generation it was impossible to impose proper industrial discipline on workers from the surrounding area. In addition,
machinery and supplies of all types had to be transported long dis-
tances.[67]

In this case, however, the general drives of American culture gradually led to the softening of local resistance. And for military reasons the
federal government kept up pressure for greater efficiency. In 1819 John
Hall, one of the most gifted machinists of the early nineteenth century,
was financed to build a special shop at the armory for making breech-
loading rifles. Designing and building most of his own machinery, he
was credited by his contemporaries with first achieving interchangeability of parts. As in the case of the high-pressure steam
engine, Hall's innovations appear to have been indigenous, involving
no important transference of European technology.[68]

While heavy ironwork, particularly after the exhaustion of surface deposits of ore, tended to center in New York and Pennsylvania, manufacturers using small quantities of iron or other metals located in all the
areas where there were laborers and skilled artisans. From the 1790s on,
industries that employed some power machinery to manufacture farm
implements and guns were established in Connecticut, Rhode Island,
and Massachusetts; being remote from large sources of iron ore, they
tended to use high-cost local supplies or to buy imported iron. The federal government gave a lift to arms manufacture in New England in
1794 by authorizing an armory or arsenal at Springfield, Massachusetts.[69] The Springfield works, in a busy mill area along the Connecticut River, had early successes quite in contrast to the troubles of

the isolated plant at Harpers Ferry. It should also be remembered that in the Connecticut Valley many private gunsmiths were supplying farmers and the state militias from local shops, and so it was easy to sub-contract special types of work, while it was not at Harpers Ferry.

In light industry the highly developed woodworking shops retarded the use of metal in clocks, textile machinery, and parts for water mills. In the lower Delaware Valley and New York City, however, iron was rapidly replacing wood by 1800. In southern New England, aside from guns, the spread of metalwork came, in general, only during and after the various interruptions to trade from 1808 to 1815. Hence wooden clocks in Connecticut in 1810 may seem a sign of backwardness, but, from a different perspective, they show the high level of perfection achieved by technology in wood.[70]

VIII

From the standpoint of useful quantification, or for the construction of mathematical models, the manufacturing statistics of 1810, 1822, or 1832 are nearly useless.[71] The census forms were so complicated and ambiguous that outside of literate New England most manufacturers brushed them aside. The 1810 figures are probably the most accurate because they were reassessed for the government by Tench Coxe of Philadelphia. An experienced civil servant and thoughtful merchant-financier Coxe would probably be correct in rank orders of the value of manufactures where the differences between classifications were over 25 percent. On this basis it is possible to determine the relative values of various types of manufacture in 1810, but even this impressionistic picture is not possible for the two later censuses or for the totals for the leading states. As would be anticipated, the rank order of products is strikingly different from that of the twentieth century.

Although the specific figures for 1810 are not reliable, nevertheless when they show that the production of leather goods, because of the need for harnesses, saddles, boots, and shoes, exceeded that of iron and steel by over 30 percent and was second only to flour milling among goods manufactured outside the home, the rank order was no doubt correct. Manufactures of food products, including liquors, were next to leather and above iron and steel. Each of these leading products—flour, leather, prepared food and drink, and iron and steel—was estimated at above $14 million annually. There was then a big drop to all types of machinery, estimated at $6.1 million, and wood products, at $5.6 million, of which ships made up about one-third. The only other major categories were hats and chemicals, estimated at over $4 million each. Textiles are missing from this list because of nearly universal home manufacture, even if the products were sold commercially. Coxe estimated the value of textile mill products, chiefly thread, at under $2 million. In ranking states from the totals, Pennsylvania was by far the largest, with total production in the range of $30 to $40 million. New York was next, with from $20 to $30 million, and Massachusetts, just short of $20 million, followed. Virginia was fourth, with a reported $11 million, and Maryland fifth at $6.5 million, but Connecticut disputed this claim.[72]

IX

The intense American interest in manufacturing, seen as a second war for independence from Britain, is illustrated by the number of associations for promoting industry and many other desired ends in all the northeastern states. Some societies for such promotion began during the Revolution, and at least two of the early ones—the Pennsylvania Society for the Encouragement of Manufactures and Useful Arts, and the New Jersey Society for Establishing Useful Manufactures—invested capital unsuccessfully in spinning mills.[73] The movement had a strong resurgence after the War of 1812. In 1817, for example, there appeared the Delaware Society for the Promotion of American Manufactures, the Philadelphia Society for the Promotion of National Industry, and, in New York, the American Society for the Encouragement of American Manufactures. Whether any of these societies accomplished much except winning some tariff increases is hard to say, but they illustrate the cooperative spirit and the strength of the desire for industrialization in the young nation.

In this early period of rapid technological and organizational change, the chief forces at work also appear to be cultural or societal, as modified of necessity by geography and resources. Artisans in all the northeastern colonies, then states, brought up in the varied needs of an expanding society, were familiar with many tools and many types of work.[74] Also critical to economic development as it proceeded was, according to Nathan Rosenberg, "a sophisticated knowledge of metallurgy and the capacity to perform precision work in metals."[75] Often significant improvements did not need new capital. Unlike European entrepreneurs who managed skilled tasks, Americans had the stimulation of the rapidly growing economy that pressed for more of everything. In the economic language of H. J. Habakkuk, "It was the interplay between constraints on the factor side and the prospects of expanding markets . . . which was the distinguishing feature of American development."[76] Diane Lindstrom sees much of the rapid growth stemming from local business efficiency.[77]

As early as 1825 Thomas Jefferson wrote, "Our manufactures are now very nearly on a footing with those of England. She has not a single improvement which we do not possess, and many of them better adapted by ourselves to our ordinary use."[78] Certainly by 1825 the first stage of the industrialization of the United States was over. While the states along the Northeast Coast were not as populous as Britain and had a less valuable annual industrial product, they manufactured all the goods necessary to lead to increasing industrial maturity. If industrialization is thought of as "revolutionary," the "revolution" had occurred. Had New York or Philadelphia capitalists been more venturesome the nation might even have had steam railroads before Britain. From this time on, American industry, reacting to its environment, produced its own dynamics, and comparisons with Britain or Europe became less important.

5
Industrial Upsurge, 1825—40

While in 1825 most of the people of the United States still lived on farms, the culture, as we have seen, possessed in abundance the technological and business knowledge and the motivation necessary for rapidly increasing industrialization. The revolutionary phase was over. In the following fifteen years the lines of development already established led to an increasingly productive economy depending more on iron and somewhat more on steam. Even in 1850 steam still cost more per horsepower than water, but it was usually necessary in cities.[1] In Philadelphia, which had the largest number of steam engines in 1838, there were thirty-four in milling, grinding, and sawing, thirty-six in textiles, and fifty-six in metals; a majority of all types were fired by coal.[2] Regardless of location or types of power, growth involved an evolution from work largely guided by a proprietor to production by a larger number of workers controlled by supervisors, a transition that made mills or shops into factories. Much the same development took place in Britain during the 1830s.[3]

I

Before the coming of the railroads, transport costs were high compared to those for capital and labor. Hence there was likely to be more immediate gain from inproving transportation than from introducing new machines or methods into production. Looked at another way, the size of a plant was limited by the size of its market, and that size depended, in part, on how far away the goods could be sold. The first phase of the "transportation revolution" necessary to provide markets for big central-ized plants depended on steamboats and trunkline canals. The unusual success of the Erie in New York, from the opening of its first section in 1819, started a canal mania that lasted two decades and led to the completion by 1840 of over three thousand miles of canals. With the help of British investment in the state bonds issued to raise the necessary money and the engineering experience gained in digging the Erie, canals were completed rapidly between 1823 and 1837. The United States could have built the canals with local capital, but not nearly as quickly as with the help of $60 million in British and other foreign subscriptions to state funds. In Europe canals had served their purpose for generations, but in America the day of the canal was over almost as soon as the big ditches were completed. Before 1845 the railroad was becoming more economical on a year-round basis than the canal. This, of course, does not mean a lack of net social gain from this investment of about $100 million in overhead capital, but within two decades, ex-cept for the Erie, all but a few short canals had been made obsolete by railroads and were no longer profitable.[4]

The timing of the canal mania in America has a fascinating irony. As early as 1809 Oliver Evans was trying to persuade Philadelphians to build a railroad. In 1811 John Stevens sent a pamphlet to all leading New York politicians, giving details of construction and exact estimates of cost for a railroad from Albany to Buffalo, but the commission study-ing the matter refused to finance even a short experimental line, and Stevens's own money was tied up in river steamboats. Partly because of canal interests in both America and Britain, the completely untested as-sumption that railroads were impractical continued to be held for some fifteen years longer by people as intelligent as Robert Livingston of New York, as well as by most British capitalists.[5]

In 1827, in spite of an increasing number of advocates of railroads, Pennsylvania, Maryland, and Ohio decided on large canal investments; by 1830, when construction of the big ditches had only begun, the steam-powered railroad had already proven its commercial viability. In theory, canals can offer cheaper transport than rails, but in fact, annual maintenance costs—repairing locks and banks damaged by ice and floods—were extremely high and the movement of inventories on horse-drawn boats, since most canals could not withstand the turbu-lence of steamboats, was extremely slow. In addition, canals suffered seasonal losses, as most shut down in winter when ice and snow blocked water passage but actually facilitated the movement of goods on turn-pikes. Among the states seeking western connections, Massachusetts was fortunate in that a trunkline canal, although seriously considered, was never attempted.

Most of the canals in the Northeast connected the backcountry with tidewater. Two canals—the Erie (1825) and the Pennsylvania Mainline (1834)—connected the Great Lakes and the Ohio Valley with the At-lantic Coast; two—the Delaware and Chesapeake (1830) and the Dela-ware and Raritan (1838) totaling about fifty miles—created a protected waterway from Long Island Sound to the Chesapeake Bay; by 1833 Lake Erie was connected with Portsmouth on the Ohio River. The previous year canals began to facilitate the movement of Pennsylvania anthracite to both New York and Philadelphia. The coal-carrying canals were profitable, except for the Morris Canal from Easton, Pennsylvania, through mountainous country to the New York City area. Profitable too, of course, was the Erie Canal. The state-owned Pennsylvania Mainline crossed the Alleghenies by thirty miles of a European-type inclined-plane railroad. While this canal system as a whole never made money, for nearly twenty years it performed the economically valuable function of connecting Philadelphia with Pittsburgh and the Ohio Val-ley. State canals started in both Indiana and Illinois were not completed before depression from 1839 on brought work to a halt.

In general the canals, only a few of which were private enterprises, represented a state subsidy, supported in part by British investors, to the growth of transportation. Their net social value cannot be measured. With some research the total loss in capital and annual deficits could be calculated, let us say to 1855, when the railroad was dominant. But the loss from diverting scarce capital from rails to water during some thirty years is too problematical for measurement.

II

In addition to the base laid by improved transportation, trade and fi-nance were unusually favorable to growth from 1823 to 1836. The sale of bonds abroad, together with the cash from mounting cotton sales to Britain, permitted large imports of commodities. The cash balances were regularly exhausted by purchases of iron and its products from Britain, Norway, Sweden, and Russia, and of luxury goods from several nations. Both types of imports probably retarded the development of domestic industry. But beyond all speculation is the fact of the more rapid growth in United States population—about 3 percent a year—and hence a steadily increasing domestic demand for goods. The demand could have been more reliable if financed by installment payments or other steady incentives, but such action, save for money raised through mortgages, was unthought of in the world of the early nineteenth century and was in part compensated for by credit terms of up to eighteen months. An expanding market also produced many entries into industry, and American optimism led to many failures, but the pressures of the in-and-out process continued to ensure, as they had in previous years, the introduction of new equipment and the weakening of traditional practices. In addition, the prejudice against American goods because of assumed careless workmanship—a prejudice fostered by importers—had by 1825 largely disappeared. [6]

For the Northeast Coast as a whole from 1825 to 1840 the outstanding feature was growth of both population and industry in New York State. During this period, in contrast to the following one, it outstripped Pennsylvania in rate of growth in population as well as in agriculture and trade. The Mohawk Valley, aided after 1825 by the completed Erie Canal, and the cities along the Hudson River came to be major farming and industrial areas. Albany and Troy, using ore from Lake Champlain, became important for ironworking, particularly in the burgeoning market for stoves and grates. New York City expanded not only as the entrepôt for foreign trade, but also as, next to Philadelphia, the most important manufacturing center. With the final completion of the Delaware and Raritan Canal in 1838, a third of the imports through the port of New York went directly on to Philadelphia through an all-water connection. Both ironworking and shipbuilding expanded in the New York metropolitan area, but aside from these activities the city was chiefly an industrial center for processing food and other consumer goods.

In this increasingly integrated northeastern economy, price fluctuations, tariffs, finance, and the business cycle all came to have more and more impact on the rhythms of life. As would be expected in an economy expanding more rapidly than any other, price fluctuations were larger than in the rest of the world. In 1819 American prices reached a high point, one equivalent to drastically lowering the cost of all imports, and one that could not be sustained. During the 1830s prices rose again to a peak in 1839, far exceeding a mild increase in British prices, and then fell 43 percent early in the next decade. [7]

Such price fluctuations alone go far to explain variations in the annual volume of various imports, but tariffs also had effects. Starting with protection for cheap cotton cloth in 1816, the tariff acts of 1818, 1824, 1828, and 1832 gave higher specific or ad valorem duties to products such as glass, wool and woolens, and metals and metal products including rolled or hammered iron.[8] Since the cost of both glass and iron were falling, specific duties, such as $37 a ton on rolled bar in 1828, gave increasingly high protection. The tariff of 1832 kept duties high on iron but lowered them on textiles, as American textiles were increasingly competitive with British textiles in world markets.[9] Then, because of the threat of secession by South Carolina, rates were reduced in the tariff act of 1833, effective in 1835, by equal annual decreases to maximum levels of 20 percent by 1842. This gradual scaling down dropped, for example, the duty on bar iron to $25 a ton.

Whether prior to the coming of the railroad the American iron industry could have grown and prospered as much as it did without some protection is impossible to judge. Except for producers selling to manufacturers in the seaport cities—and that is a big exception, particularly in the case of New England—freight rate protection was an important factor. With the high tariff of 1828 in force, about one-quarter of the bar iron, or under one-fifth of all iron used, was imported. The imports were only in small part from Britain, whose iron accounted for merely 2.6 percent of total imports from 1827 to 1830.[10] Most of the importation was through New England ports remote from the New York or Pennsylvania sources of ore. Certainly an iron industry of about the same size would have developed in any case in central Pennsylvania. Or, in broader terms, industrialization seemed bound to advance in the United States on the basis of culture, geography, and resources regardless of foreign competition, but the pace and forms of advance were influenced by public policies.

Later history has illustrated that as industrialization creates a demand for increasingly specialized products, the interchange between advanced nations becomes ever more complex. Nathan Trotter, a metal importer of Philadelphia, was quick to change from imports to domestic products, or vice versa, as tariffs and qualities altered. For example, protection for brazier's copper in the tariff of 1816 encouraged domestic production, and in 1822 Trotter started buying in Baltimore. He also claimed that the domestic product was of better quality than the British. At the same time, however, he imported copper sheathing. Tariff increases on brass up to 1833 led Trotter to turn to a Waterbury, Connecticut, firm. For brass wire, however, he bought in Easton, Pennsylvania. Antiquated methods of making brass kettles in England in the 1830s opened this metals market to mechanized American producers.[11]

III

In addition to the strong effect of trade and tariff policies on transportation and manufactures, the banking policies of both states and nation also stimulated capital investment from 1825 to 1837.[12] On the national level the decade after 1825 was an unusually favorable one in American banking. The Second Bank of the United States (BUS), with Nicholas Biddle as president from 1823 on, kept state bank issues on a reasonably sound but expanding basis by the occasional threat of demanding large note redemptions. The BUS also facilitated internal trade and demand by transferring funds as required from one part of the nation to another and by providing foreign exchange. It did not perform the central banking function of being a lender of last resort in times of crisis, but during the rest of its federal charter, which ended in 1836, there was no great need for this function.[13] Banks continued to grow in number, from 506 in 1834 to 901 in 1840, and to produce an increasing volume of credit up to 1837, but such overexpansion, probably inevitable in a unit banking system during a long period of rising prices and general prosperity, undoubtedly stimulated industrial investment.[14]

Thus, during this fifteen-year period the American banking system appears to have been a positive factor in both industrial and general economic growth, although perhaps not many bankers consciously took on the development function. Insofar as practically all banks renewed accommodation loans (those secured only by personal signatures) over and over again for people in whom the directors had confidence, these sums became part of the capital structure of enterprise, just as though the banks had subscribed to stocks or bonds.

The troubles in the banking world from 1836 on came from changes brought about by a combination of federal policy and external forces. Hostility of state bankers, the opposition or lukewarm support of New York financial interests for a Philadelphia institution, and personal animosity between Biddle and President Jackson combined to prevent the recharter of the BUS. In consequence, the bank was forced to pay an exorbitant price in bonuses and subscriptions to state enterprises to get a Pennsylvania charter. Even so, the BUS was still the largest bank but it was deprived of handling federal funds and had no reason to feel responsible for the soundness of banking policies. Meanwhile, mounting tariff revenues had paid off the national debt, and starting in 1836 the federal government deposited surplus cash in selected state banks. According to a recent analysis, the resulting increase in bank reserves was important only in softening the impact of the crisis of 1837.[15]

While in a nation growing as rapidly as the United States in the early 1830s every boom is likely to overheat the economy and end in a severe crisis, the two crisis years of 1837 and 1839 terminated the period of foreign investment in state bonds to aid transportation and depended for their timing largely on British actions. The decade from 1826 to 1835 was a period of sharply rising cotton exports, totaling in value about two-thirds more than in the previous ten years and in 1836, at $71 million, establishing a record for the period before 1850. This staple for international payments gave British investors confidence in American state bonds, which yielded much more than their own government securities. So the boom went forward on American exports of cotton and British exports of capital. With both canal and railroad building pushed by state and private enterprise, and with credit easy to secure, labor became scarce and prices rose rapidly.

At the beginning of 1836 the Bank of England became worried by a drain of gold that was assumed to be to the United States and stopped rediscounting the paper of the chief cotton importing houses. In other words, it sought to limit advances of mercantile credit to the United States. This action, rather than President Jackson's calling for specie payment for public lands, started the credit squeeze that broke the boom. The recession was mild, however, and with expansion of credit by the banks receiving federal deposits and with borrowing by the BUS to hold cotton off the market, there was recovery in 1838.[16] If the cotton crop of 1839 had been small and the wheat crop large, Biddle's scheme for boosting cotton export prices might have succeeded, but the case was exactly the reverse. The United States could not supply the unusual British requirement for wheat, while the cotton crop overflowed the means available for keeping it off the market.

The collapse of 1839 was in the beginning more a trade than a banking crisis, but by this time states and private investors were being forced to cut back sharply on the construction of canals and railroads, unfinished sections were losing money, and all the pessimism associated with deep depression set in. In 1841 the BUS failed, and a half a dozen states, including Pennsylvania, defaulted on payment of interest on their bonds. Revival came in 1843 only after a 43 percent decline in United States prices since 1839.

IV

Long-run economic or technological change was often little affected by financial fluctuations, however. The orienting of farmers to urban markets, for example, encouraged better practices, and the development of new agricultural machinery made more important contributions to the rate of industrial growth. Together these developments created a frontier of potential change in agriculture as well as increasing supplies for industrial cities. The hinterland farms near the big cities became capable of providing food for many more urban workers and still were able to leave their young people free to migrate east or west.

In 1790 American farming practices had scarcely changed from the days of initial settlement. Cities and towns had grown slowly, and, except for coastwise or river trade in some staples, food was drawn only from nearby expanding farm areas. With an abundance of land, rough balances had been struck whereby farms in the vicinity of metropolitan areas produced a sufficient surplus without needing to employ methods for maintaining the soil. Educated gentlemen boasted of generations of cultivation without attempts to restore fertility. Even in regions where farmers could readily sell their surplus produce the pattern of cultivation was much the same as on the self-sufficient frontier farm; metropolitan area farms differed only in planting some extra acres in market crops like fruits, vegetables, corn, or wheat. Vegetable farming and fruit growing were also done in the cities, even in the major metropolises, with gardens and orchards set in the backyards of houses fronting on streets. [17]

But the results of nearly a century of farming as though still on the frontier of settlement were deplorable. Land was overcropped, with little effort to restore fertility; manure was wasted; and top soil often washed from high spots and sunk in undrained gullies. Many gentlemen farmers knew of the English practices of rotation of crops and the application of calcium fertilizers and manure, and they tried some of these methods on their farms. But in contrast to city artisans, where a convergence of shops within a few blocks forced skilled craftsmen to learn from each other in order to compete, farmers felt little pressure to seek or trade information. [18] In industry a score of entrepreneurs could set a pattern, while among the millions of farmers leaders were easily obscured. The one good farmer in a hundred had little effect on his neighbors, chiefly because he lived apart and usually moved in different social and economic circles.

The tendency to invest in new land, instead of in improvement of the soil or in purchase of machinery, was an important factor retarding the general advance of farm practices. The extreme of this tendency can be seen in Virginia, where even such men as Thomas Jefferson brought new acreage into production and completely abandoned worn-out fields. Insofar as the motive for buying land was to resell at a higher price, industrialization increased the tendency along the whole Northeast Coast. Provision for growing families and protection against soil exhaustion were also motives for buying excess land. Investment in fertilizer, tools, or machinery was seen as a risk; it might pay for itself or it might not, whereas land seemed a gilt-edged security. Consequently average farmers, even some near major industrial centers, responded slowly and reluctantly to putting cash into either more labor, more supplies, or new equipment.

The very backwardness of agriculture in 1790 was in one way a spur to rapid American industrialization. There was a vast store of agricultural knowledge waiting to be drawn on, and even small improvements—and they did come in response to higher local demand—substantially increased the productivity of those farms feeding the big cities. In the long run Percy Wells Bidwell and John I. Falconer, the classic historians of northern agriculture, are correct in saying, "Had the new farm tools and machines not appeared manufactures would have been checked by rising labor costs."[19] In fact, food production easily kept pace with demand, and farm wages often lagged behind price changes caused by outside forces.[20]

When trade and manufacturing sped the rapid growth of the seaport cities, and hard-surfaced roads reached into the hinterland, workers were drawn from farms at the same time that urban demand for food rapidly increased. For farmers within reach of city markets, agriculture suddenly became a business. Thus industrialization did what no amount of literature or lecturing by agricultural societies had been able to accomplish. The farmer, faced with loss of family labor to city jobs and the chance for increased cash income from more production, met his problem in the same way as the urban businessman: he specialized, took poor land out of cultivation, and employed new methods.[21] As might be expected, the improvements from the 1790s on were most advanced around the leading seaports, particularly Boston, New York, and Philadelphia. The Philadelphia Society for Promoting Agriculture, the New York Board of Agriculture, and the Massachusetts Agricultural Society took the lead in promoting rotation of crops.[22] But every growing inland town or city, such as Worcester, Albany, or Lancaster, generated a pressure for improved agriculture, and agricultural journals circulated widely. Because of demand, climate, and fertility, the lower Delaware Valley counties became the leaders of the nation in new practices, technology, and increased productivity.

In all of the ensuing improvements in methods and machines, the demands of the export trade played a negligible role. As foreign nations strove to be agriculturally self-sufficient and West Indian demand stabilized, there was little change in the combined volume of wheat and flour exports from 1790 to 1840 and a 40 percent drop in those of corn.[23] During the same period northeastern urban consumption grew about tenfold. As Clarence H. Danhof has observed, "The urban consuming population and the capacity of farmers to place their products on the market grew in such close relationship as to relegate overseas markets to a buffer role."[24]

The large number of semiliterate farmer-entrepreneurs—many of them tenants—and their separation from each other made for a slow and uneven spread of all new techniques.[25] The dominant factors in forcing farmers to move from the traditional practices of the geographic frontier to the modern methods of the frontier of change were access to markets and the pressure of demand. Together these factors raised the price of the farmer's land to a point that induced him to sell if he could not improve his methods. In Massachusetts, where the soil was thin and had been cropped for many years, there were fairly well recognized areas outside of which it did not pay to produce for market, except perhaps in the form of cider or whiskey.[26] For such farmers, and for their counterparts in other states, income was low, life was hard, and most children went west or to the city.

The earliest improvements were in fertilization and rotation of crops. Better conservation and the application of manure and wood ashes (potash) came early and were followed by the use of powdered gypsum, called plaster of paris (calcium sulfate) and in later years properly treated lime (calcium oxide).[27] Between 1790 and 1820 all these practices helped to restore the fertility of the soil in metropolitan area acreages such as Delaware and Chester counties in Pennsylvania, Dutchess and Westchester counties in New York, and Suffolk County in Massachusetts. Crop rotations of varying complexity evolved, but all depended on plowing under crops of red clover or timothy to restore soil nitrates and on assigning land periodically to cattle grazing. The famous Chester County (Pennsylvania) System involved rotating wheat, oats or rye, corn, clover or timothy, grass, and cattle over a ten-year period. But the spread of such systems was slow because soil exhaustion from wheat and corn showed only gradually, and change could always be put off for another year.[28]

There were some improvements in the raising of livestock. The original stock of Devon cattle brought from England had deteriorated over the years from a combination of inadequate shelter, insufficient feeding in winter months, and lack of selective breeding. From the 1820s on, Ayrshires and other new breeds were imported and given better care.[29] Similar improvements were introduced in breeds of pigs and sheep.

Changes in tools and farm machinery represent the direct entrance of industrialization into agriculture. For centuries there had been little technological advance save for the cradle partially replacing the scythe in harvesting wheat. After 1800 there were new patents taken out every year on agricultural machines or implements, and in some years a good many. One could say that there was an industrial revolution in agricultural technology, but the pracitcal application of machinery, like the application of new methods, was slow and uneven.

Up to 1815 improvements were chiefly in better hand tools; then a period of continuous mechanical improvement began. While in Pennsylvania cast iron plows went back to 1797, they did not spread until 1817 when Jethro Wood of New York City began producing them with replaceable parts, the first example of the idea of interchangeability in agriculture.[30] These better-shaped iron plows made possible deeper furrows with less ox power. The hay rake available in 1823 was perhaps the major labor-saving device of the age, for it allowed a man, a boy, and a horse to do the work of six men and one or two oxen.[31] The substitution after 1820 of the more expensive but quicker horse for the slow-plodding ox in New York and Pennsylvania made the new machines far more effective in saving time and labor. In addition, wheel harrows, seed drills, and mechanical threshers were all available by the middle of the 1820s, but outside of the lower Delaware Valley the new devices were not widely adopted before 1840. The following decade saw the more general adoption of machinery, which by this time was well tested through use on the more advanced farms. Yet, even by 1850 probably less than a quarter of the farmers in the Northeast used modern methods and equipment.[32] Even in advanced areas, such as those supplying the major cities, American yields compared to English were still low per acre, but high per worker.

Far more Americans worked on farms than in shops or factories, so a small decrease in the need for agricultural labor could greatly affect the urban labor market. Conversely, the increasing number of farm jobs as agriculture expanded—about 30 to 50 percent of farms in the northern states had a hired hand—kept farm wages rising during the period from 1800 to 1840 and helped to put a floor under the rates for unskilled factory labor.

A further supply of urban workers from domestic farms came with the gradual termination of household industries between 1810 and 1850. As the farmer became able to sell crops in the town or city markets, he could buy an increasing number of the things previously made at home for less than their cost in family board and labor. This development released unneeded family members for migration to new farms or the urban labor market. At the same time a decline in fertility in the older areas reduced the initial size of farm families, which, in turn, increased the acreage that could be used for market crops instead of for subsistence.[33]

From pre-Revolutionary times some family farms close to cities were involved in spinning and weaving textiles on order for urban merchants. While cotton spinning for the market had generally moved to factories by 1815, cotton weaving remained a household industry in some areas into the 1850s.[34] New Yorkers in 1825 produced nine yards of household cloth per capita; in 1845 the amount was less than three yards.[35] Both movements were slower in woolens, which barely entered factory production until after 1815.[36] When production was moved to the factory, the same workers might either go with it or turn to increased farm production.

Thus the process of shifting from household to shop or mill, although said to be as revolutionary to rural life as the growth of industrialization was to wage earners, went on in the United States without real hardship; there was always extra acreage for male children to cultivate, frequently as tenant farmers, and a rapidly expanding industrial system to absorb both male and female labor.[37] By way of contrast, in some European nations, where all available land was already in cultivation and industrial expansion was slow, the factory pressure on household industry produced underemployment on farms and consequent rural impoverishment.

V

In the period after 1825 the geographical outlines of the location of heavy industry and metalwork that were to last until well past mid-century emerged. The backbone of production ran from Albany and Troy down the Hudson Valley, embracing many small-city plants, to New York; it shifted westward from Paterson to Trenton, New Jersey, and then ran down the Delaware River beyond Wilmington and into Maryland. In the West heavy industry for local needs followed the Ohio from Pittsburgh to Cincinnati.

Up to 1820 the big cities had grown the fastest; from then on practically all cities began a period of rapid growth. Consequently, urban household expenditures, which had been less than a third of the national total in 1820, came to nearly half of a much larger total two decades later.[38] In the newer industries the major metropolitan areas developed specialties based on resources and types of trade. Among the port cities only Baltimore and Philadelphia generated more income from value added in manufacturing than from trade, but most other cities had the largest portion of their labor force engaged in plants and factories.[39]

Greater Philadelphia was the major center for metalwork, including pipes, stoves, and castings, but the New York metropolitan area was close behind. In contrast to the limited regions producing heavy industry, consumer goods were produced everywhere in the northeastern states from Maryland to Maine and New Jersey to Ohio; the interior markets were chiefly for American-made goods. Manufacture of fine textiles such as ginghams, woolens, and carpets was centered at Philadelphia, cheap textiles in Rhode Island and eastern Massachusetts, and trade in their specialties went on regularly between these two sections.[40] Metal manufacturing for household use, including guns, grew in all centers of population, but particularly in New York and Connecticut. Leather manufactures, very important in the days of saddles and harnesses, went on in all states from hides tanned largely in New York and Pennsylvania. The same wide dispersion was true of woodworking, furniture making, and carriage building. While in 1840 the coastal states from New York to Virginia still milled 57 percent of the total flour—the nation's chief manufacturing process—the center of the industry was moving westward from upstate New York to the Ohio Valley and the Great Lakes.

Oddly enough, statistics on manufacturing output for 1825–40 are even more unreliable than for the previous fifteen years because there is no equivalent of Tench Coxe's estimates of 1810. Neither of the special censuses of manufactures for 1822 or 1832 have any validity outside of New England, and, in spite of some improvements, manufactures were not reliably recorded in the census of 1840. A special report from the secretary of state to the United States Senate in 1824 on the value of domestic manufacture of dutiable articles also presents a table of dubious accuracy. In this report, as in every other record, Pennsylvania ranks first and New York a close second, but then Ohio is third, Virginia fourth, Connecticut fifth, and Massachusetts sixth. Although by this time most manufactures, including textiles, were dutiable, the departure from the usual ranking of Pennsylvania, New York, and Massachusetts undoubtedly represents not only the influence of iron interests but also the skewed nature typical of the returns.[41]

The industrializing region of the Northeast was its own best customer. In the period 1825 to 1840 less than one-fifth of its manufactures left the area. The big trade of the region was intraregional around the urban areas of high income and consumption. In the case of the largest manufacturing center, Philadelphia, its demand was primarily from its own local area. Aside from the surrounding counties the best customers for goods manufactured in Philadelphia were in New York City.[42]

From Pittsburgh down the Ohio and from Buffalo out across the Great Lakes, the West was industrializing, but to a large eextent on a self-sufficient basis. Some grain and meat was shipped east, but tonnage eastward on the Erie Canal to tidewater in the boom year of 1836 was still over 80 percent in-state.[43] While Cincinnati and Pittsburgh were well developed in heavy industry, they used iron from western Pennsylvania to build their own steam engines in river boats and built factories for consumer goods that took care of local needs. Some of their boats and raw materials were exported through New Orleans.

For scholars brought up on Britain's need to export, a largely self-sufficient industrial revolution in America requires a readjustment in concepts. Certainly the American market grew, but it grew from immigration, high domestic fertility, and rising local income both agricultural and industrial. For example, while New York and Pennsylvania benefited from flour and coal exports to other regions in the Western hemisphere and trade with other sections of the United States, had the two states been completely isolated they would still have industrialized rapidly.

VI

As Phyllis Deane has written, "The first industrial revolution grew upon a basis of coal and iron."[44] By 1825 practically all durable and up-to-date machinery was made from iron, or its derivative steel, and railroad tracks, bridges, and eventually even large buildings required iron. Ore and pig varied greatly in their qualities, and the chemistry involved was still a mystery. In general, for further working, hammered bar iron was still superior to puddled and rolled iron, but for use in sheets or rails the latter was acceptable. Once a manufacturer found a satisfactory iron he was inclined to continue to use it regardless of small fluctuations in price. In spite of high tariff duties, superior quality bar iron—the type desired by many manufacturers—could be imported more cheaply from Norway, Sweden, and Russia than an equivalent domestic product could sell for in the port cities remote from the mines. But in the ore-producing inland areas and the nearest ports, the lower transportation costs balanced the lower labor costs of foreign forges. While Swedish or Russian pig was superior for some purposes, American charcoal smelting produced good malleable iron, equal for most purposes to the imports and preferred to iron from British coke smelters. Coal was not essential in the United States until near mid-century. Even though located in Philadelphia, where there was easy access to imports, Baldwin Locomotive Company and other big iron users dealt with Pennsylvania suppliers who used charcoal.[45]

By 1825 the widely scattered deposits of bog iron had been nearly exhausted, and lasting supplies of deeper ore were coming chiefly from around Lake Champlain in New York, both eastern and western Pennsylvania, and in smaller quantities from Maryland and Virginia. Estimates for 1830 place total domestic pig at 192,000 tons, with cast iron at 28,000 tons and bar iron at 96,600. Imports, chiefly bar, to Massachusetts and Maine, were 33,000 tons.[46] While Russian and Swedish iron was used, particularly for making steel and cutting tools, these figures showing imports at less than one-fifth of the total illustrate the domestic character of the iron industry.

Ironworking in blacksmith and other small shops for local consumption was a large part of the total, but the sizable works with from fifty to six or seven hundred employees were in the Albany-Troy, New York City, Philadelphia-Wilmington, and Baltimore areas. Some of their machine products were competitive with British products in the world market.[47] As Juniata ore from central Pennsylvania, with fewer impurities than that from the eastern part of the state, came through the canals, more steelmaking was attempted. In the early 1830s Philadelphia and New York City each had three steel furnaces, and there were others rather widely scattered in the northeastern states. Heat-resistant clay, necessary for both the crucible or cementation processes, was originally from Chester County, Pennsylvania. The same clay also made fine porcelain.

There were still only two main ways of making pig into iron for use by machine builders: hammering or puddling and rolling. Since rolled iron was not as good for further working as hammered iron, and since the United States had plenty of waterpower for trip-hammers, the puddling and rolling process never became important in the domestic industry until the days of rapid expansion of demand from railroads and river steamboats.[48]

As time went on, the cost of producing iron in Britain by the use of coke at all stages became lower than the cost of production by use of charcoal in the United States. There was no good coking coal east of the Alleghenies, and the great Connellsville deposits near Pittsburgh were tapped successfully only after 1850. Lack of good coking bituminous coal put a premium on finding a way to use the abundant anthractie of eastern Pennsylvania directly (without coking) for smelting and refining.

Since Scotland and Wales also had large deposits of hard coal, experiments there showed the theoretical possibility of a hot blast igniting and sustaining the combustion of anthracite in the smelting furnace. Although steam was generated from anthracite at the Phoenixville, Pennsylvania ironworks in 1825, experiments with Scotch and Welsh methods of smelting then and in the early 1830s were unsuccessful, partly from bad luck and partly from lack of capital.[49] In 1835 the Franklin Institute in Philadelphia offered a medal for successful anthracite smelting, and shortly thereafter Nicholas Biddle and his friends added a cash prize of $5,000 for three months of sustained production.[50] The ultimate success followed the frequent pattern of innovation by a British worker in an American company, in this case

Perry working in Pottsville, Pennsylvania. Presenting the
e Port Carbon Hotel in 1839, Nicholas Biddle called the
.... 'Second American Revolution" from Britain. Actually, had
Perry not succeeded, a second Welshman, George Crane, would have
probably done so within a few months at a nearby iron furnace.
Anthractie smelting necessarily involved new problems that had to be
solved by rule of thumb, and consequently replaced the use of charcoal
only gradually.

VII

A broadly competent machine tool industry appears to be essential to
continuous industrial growth. As most textile mills brought in mechanics who built their largely wooden machinery on the spot, there
were only a few specialized shops selling all types of spinning and weaving equipment to the trade. Some of the big mills also sold machinery.[51] After 1830 a specialized machinery industry grew mainly
from the demands of railroad and boat builders; it turned a good
number of the old general ironworks into specialized shops. The manufacture of railroad equipment itself, which might be categorized as either durable goods or as, tools for making tools, became a strong force
in creating specialized machinery plants.

It has been claimed by a historian of American technology that the
United States led the world in advances in steam from 1820 to 1870,[52]
and locomotives certainly exhibit an amazingly quick American success. The skepticism of the years from 1810 to 1827 was overcome by
the commercial profitability of British steam railways. Poor old John
Stevens, who had demonstrated the practicality of the steam locomotive
on an experimental scale on his estate in Hoboken a full decade before
the first steam engine on an American commercial railroad, was forgotten in the rush to manufacture lightweight locomotives for cheaply laid
tracks. It was this need for lightness that led to American innovation.
British locomotives were heavy and resisted sharp curves. By 1831
American works from West Point to Philadelphia were turning out
lightweight locomotives that could maneuver the curves without wreck-
ing the tracks.

The quick triumph of American locomotives in the home market,
and by the mid-1830s in the European market as well, was not the
result of one particular individual's ability but a consequence of the
high level of technological knowledge and practical mechanical skills of

many men living on the frontiers of change in the United States of 1830. Without consultation, as far as the present record goes, less-heralded mechanics such as Samuel Hall at the West Point Iron Works and well-known innovators like Mathias Baldwin and William Norris in Philadelphia all turned at once to building successful locomotives. Baldwin best exemplifies the all-purpose skills that could be achieved by the intelligent master mechanic of the age. A Philadephian who had been a calico printer and general machinery maker, he built a model locomotive for Peale's Museum in Independence Hall and then success-fully completed an order for a full-sized one for the Germantown and Philadelphia Railroad. Of the first 145 locomotives built by Norris, who started within a few months of Baldwin, 41 were sold abroad, including 10 in Britain. By the end of the decade other American builders were getting British orders for their locomotives, which were more adaptable to lightly constructed roads.[53]

This ready production and rapid improvement of the locomotive also illustrates the relative simplicity of early technology. Machines could be understood by master mechanics from observation and be modified to meet new requirements. A century later college-trained engineers work-ing from complete plans might find it difficult or impossible to replicate an alien machine like a household refrigerator condenser.[54]

Railroads using steam locomotives spread rapidly in the 1830s. They ran west from the major ports and north and south in the Philadel-phia–New York region, but the nearly three thousand miles of track completed by 1840 still did not provide continuous rail connections be-tween the major port cities. The economic effects, therefore, were to knit intraregional businesses closer together and speed local orders and exchanges of information. Like the electric telegraph, an innovation of the mid-1830s, the railroad's great interregional effect on transpor-tation and communication was to come between 1840 and 1854.

An immediate effect of the railroad was in the demand for equipment that, meant, in turn, the growth of more specialized machine tool fac-tories. Factories building engine parts, boilers, frames, axles, and wheels, and the lathes, drills, and other machines necessary to build them, all grew rapidly around the major cities but particularly in the Philadelphia-Wilmington area. In these machine tools the United States kept pace, at least, with Britain. G. E. Sellers of the famous ma-chinery family of Philadelphia, visiting England in 1832, found British "lathes and other machine tools . . . totally inadequate for the character of the work they had to do, as to weight strength and firmness." He thought them inferior to those made in Baltimore and Philadelphia at least six years earlier. One may make some allowance for Sellers's national chauvinism, a trait very noticeable in American culture, but his reputation for strict honesty gives weight to his statement: "Mr. Donkin [a manufacturer at Bermondsey] said if I would come to his shop . . . he thought he could show me a shop that had abandoned fixed old ways and made fair advances . . . if it has not kept up with America."[55] As early as 1828 a Prussian buyer is said to have preferred American to British machinery.[56] Such views were not shared by British economists or literary men, who still assumed they had an enormous lead in machine tools.

In substituting machines for labor Americans made many improvements and innovations. The improved slide lathe was an American invention, and filing jigs, gear cutters, milling, and other machines developed in the United States independently of foreign influence. Stationary and marine engines also stimulated the tool industry. In Rhode Island, for example, factory steam engines did more to create an ironworking industry than did boats or railroads.[57] In general, New England excelled in light metalwork and Pennsylvania in products requiring metallurgy and advanced engineering.[58] The United States, chiefly in New York and Philadelphia, produced about half its consumption of steel.

In spite of this great upswing in the demand for tools and parts from 1829 on, cast iron in volume and gunmaking for its machines continued to dominate the working of ferrous metals. Iron stoves had replaced fireplaces for both cooking and heating and, together with other cast iron products such as pipe, were made chiefly from Troy to Wilmington. Cast iron also came to be increasingly used for pillars and beams in buildings and reinforcements in ships. American gunmakers, with their great domestic market, had a world reputation by 1825 and were receiving foreign military orders.[59] The industry was centered in Connecticut, with an extension northward to the government armory at Springfield, Massachusetts. More and more of the work of manufacturing a rifle was done by machinery, and continuous, partly successful efforts were made from 1815 on, in both federal and private arsenals, to make patterns uniform and parts interchangeable.

As we have seen, the most successful early effort at interchangeability came at Harpers Ferry Armory, where the difficulties arising from the remoteness of other toolmakers and local hostility to industrial discipline continued to keep general efficiency markedly lower than at the federal arsenal at Springfield. By 1830 John Hall's separate works at Harpers Ferry were regarded as the best in the country and produced practically interchangeable parts. Robert S. Woodbury has asserted that "modern interchangeable manufacture derives far more from his inventive genius at Harpers Ferry than from Eli Whitney's manufactory at Mill Rock."[60] Perhaps too much attention has been given to interchangeability, which was a widely shared eighteenth-century European goal and which up to at least 1860 was never achieved without considerable filing of parts. The major road to efficiency in these big gun factories was extreme division of labor; a hundred tasks or stages of production were defined at Springfield by the 1820s.

Although mechanized textile manufacture was to be a by-product rather than an essential element in the rise of modern industrialization, the increasing scale of such operations and attendant management and labor problems placed cotton mills, particularly, on the frontiers of social change brought about by the factory. Up to 1810 Massachusetts had been relatively slow in turning to manufacturing. Only with the demonstration of success by Lowell, Appleton, and others at Waltham and with the later use of the great waterpower of the Merrimack River was there a large movement of capital from commerce to industry. Throughout this and the earlier period Philadelphia continued as the main center for better-grade textiles. After 1815 the Philadelphia area superseded Rhode Island as the chief producer of cotton yarn as well as of finer printed cotton cloth. By 1825 ingrain woolen carpets were being manufactured in Philadelphia on Jacquard automatic looms, and the area continued to produce as much carpet as all the rest of the nation combined.[61] Aside from coarse goods such as carpets, it was hard for large integrated American manufacturers paying more for both raw materials and labor to compete with fine British woolens, but small specialized operations using much family labor could succeed.[62]

As in many other types of manufacture, improvements in cotton textile machinery took different courses in Britain and the United States. In spinning John Thorp of Providence and William Mason of Taunton, Massachusetts, respectively, invented and perfected ring-and-cap spinning that allowed the spindles of an Arkwright frame to turn three times as fast. While this advance reduced the price of coarse cloth, it was not copied by the British because their big mills spun by mules. Instead, they perfected the self-acting mule about 1830. It could spin finer thread than cap-and-ring machines, but was not adopted in the United States before 1840. The power loom rapidly replaced handweaving in both nations after 1820, but in the United States one man tended two double power looms while it was reported that in Britain there was one worker for each machine. In addition, there was a steady impetus in the United States for increasing the speed of looms. Robert Gersed near Philadelphia doubled the speed of his looms between 1837 and 1840. Chiefly because of American pressures for economy, coarse cotton cloth, mainly from Massachusetts mills, could sell by 1830 in the Far East and Latin America in competition with similar British products. During the 1830s commercial handweaving largely disappeared in the United States, and the very fine fabrics that could not be woven by machine were imported from Britain or other countries in Europe.[63]

As would be expected in a rapidly industrializing region, in the United States the older forms of manufacture, part handicraft and part factory, continued to grow, although development was by no means uniform or even. In general chemicals, clay products, and pharmaceuticals, together with carriage building, grew fastest in southeastern Pennsylvania. Imports of chemicals exceeded home production, but most of the latter came from Philadelphia.[64] Shipbuilding and woodworking throve from there northward to Maine. In general such enterprises were small, but a few employed over five hundred workers.

VIII

In the years before 1820 the United States had become firmly set on the road to modern industrialization; twenty years later, by the standards of that day, the nation was industrialized. Interchanges of goods with Britain and Europe were those to be expected between mature industrial nations, each exporting products that because of labor costs or natural resources could be grown or made more cheaply than in the other nation. The United States had basic coal, iron, and machinery industries operated by both immigrant and native-born entrepreneurs and mechanics, men who were on the frontiers of technological change. Looking back, we may find it inconceivable that their progress could have been permanently checked.

As I argued earlier, this rapid extension of both social and technical frontiers was basically a result of culture, geography, and resources, but the specific means by which the industrial system evolved is particularly well illustrated in the two decades that ended in 1840. Writing of the

British industrial revolution, Phyllis Deane and Peter Mathias both stress the importance of the demand generated by international trade.[65] Studying the Philadelphia area in particular, however, Diane Lindstrom sees a self-reinforcing process of local development, one that would apply equally well to the New York or other major city regions.

Lindstrom's thesis is that new agricultural demand for nonfarm products increased as migration and improved transportation brought new hinterland areas in the Middle States into the sphere of urban markets. As hitherto partially idle farm youths came to work in the cities, agricultural productivity was increased by the incentives of demand, by better practices, and by new machinery; their increased productivity made it possible for farmers to consume more urban products. Another rapid increase in demand was in urban consumption itself, from the needs of thousands of new workers sustained by cheap food products from the hinterland.[66]

In short, in such naturally endowed areas as the valleys of New York and Pennsylvania, given the impetus of American culture, foreign or even intersectional trade was not essential to early industrialization.

In the years from the tariffs of 1816 and 1818 through 1835, the effective date of the compromise tariff of 1833, federal policy probably aided iron, glass, and textile manufacture. Expansive banking pracitces from 1825 to 1839 were also stimulating growth, perhaps overly so, but any control of so rapidly expanding an economy would have been difficult. Compared to England, for example, the pace of canal building in the United States was extremely rapid. The Mainline Canal and rail system between Philadelphia and Pittsburgh was completed in less than half a dozen years, and the equally long Erie Canal in eight. In contrast, the canal from the Worsley mines outside of Manchester to Liverpool took fifteen years to finish and the one from Leeds to Liverpoor forty-six.[67] Not all American canals were completed as quickly per mile as the Erie and the Mainline, but the capital burden of building both canals and railroads simultaneously in the 1830s could only be supported by foreign investment.

The resulting financial dramatics of the period, enhanced in history texts by such colorful figures as Nicholas Biddle and Andrew Jackson, obscure the underlying physical progress from 1826 to 1839 in transportation, agriculture, and industry. The change in transportation ultimately brought about by railroads could have come earlier, save for the conservatism of both British and American investors. In both nations

,powered railroads were vigorously urged by innovative technical / from 1803 on, but only with the use of steam on the British Stockton and Darlington in 1827 were capitalist converts made to investment in extensive construction. By world standards Britain and the United States innovated the steam railroad in the 1820s and 1830s, but judged by internal possibilities both nations built such roads gradually.[68]

Hence the phase of the transportation revolution before 1840 was much more dependent on turnpikes, canals, and steamboats than on rails. Cheaper transportation gradually ended the self-sufficient character of industrialization around the major cities and encouraged regional specialization with larger-scale production.

6
Industrial Maturity, 1840- ⌐

The rapid development of the Northeast Coast in the mid-1840s marks the end of the pioneer stage of industrialization, that of the creation of the early prototypes of modern machines producing largely for regional economies. The late 1830s began a period during which the continuing drives of American culture made the nation, in fact if not in reputation, the world leader in the application of machinery to mass production. While by 1838 canals connected Baltimore with New York, railroads gradually opened still more interregional markets to firms able to compete successfully. [1]

I

The success of railroads depended on efficient steam engines. The early high-pressure engines of Oliver Evans, Richard Trevithick, and others lacked the efficiency that came from George Stephenson's and Timothy Hackworth's simultaneous development in 1810 of the steam exhaust blast to increase the draft under boilers. But even with theoretically viable locomotives, merchant capitalists, the main source of funds in both countries, doubted the ability of iron wheels depending for their traction on friction with iron rails to generate enough pulling power to rival the cost of transport by canals or even wagons on turnpikes. In the British Parliament the canal lobby was powerful enough to hold up a charter for the Stockton and Darlington Railway from 1819 to 1823. And when the railroad was completed in 1825, steam locomotives were used only on a few level stretches. Not until Stephenson demonstrated his newly designed *Rocket* at the Rainhill trials, sponsored in 1829 by the Liverpool and Manchester Railway to determine their future motive power, was the steam locomotive accepted by hard-headed financiers.[2]

Meanwhile much the same interplay between reluctant capitalists, canal interests, and overoptimistic innovators was going on in the United States. John Stevens's correspondence with Robert Livingston and the New York State canal commissioners in 1812 illustrates the combination of technological uncertainty and heavy capital costs that held back the steam railroad. Even a short trial line would involve untried technology and substantial capital. Furthermore, every part of the equipment would have to be put to new uses. Mine railways had operated at no more than the speed of a walking horse. Up to 1825, no steam-propelled vehicle designed by Evans, Stevens, Trevithick, Stephenson, or others had performed in commercial transportation service. In America snow and frost had proven severe problems for turnpikes and canals and threatened the same for railroads. To avoid damage from frost Stevens proposed elevating the tracks on wooden poles projecting four feet from the ground. He thought wooden rails would stand the wear, but, if not, "cast or plated iron rail-ways . . . could be fastened to the top of the wooden." Obviously this particular roadbed would have had to be modified. Although Livingston may have opposed the railroad partly because of his interest in steamboats, one can sympathize with his and Gouverneur Morris's objections on the basis of the proposed technology. After a battle with canal and turnpike interests in New Jersey, Stevens won a state charter for a railroad from Trenton to New Brunswick in 1815; eight years later he chartered the Pennsylvania Railroad.[3] In neither case could he raise enough capital to begin a road. Such conservatism on the part of merchant capitalists may seem amazing. But by the time steam finally won out in Britain, American capital was in general more plentiful and potential rail traffic larger, and Americans were ready to risk money in railroads. Thus the ultimate actions were the result of mounting demand and supply rather than any spectacular technological breakthrough.

Elaborate British methods of construction were obviously not suited to the longer roads through sparsely populated areas needed in the United States. Just as American mill architects were substituting leather belting for gear wheels, American railroad "engineers" substituted wood cross-ties for granite blocks and wooden-based strap rails for completely metal ones. The use of wood for cross-ties turned out to be the lasting solution; the strap rails were not. But each experiment was generically of the same basic type. American culture was highly oriented to the future. Builders were "go ahead people" who made do with what they had.[4] They knew they were building too cheaply, but they reasoned that when traffic demanded replacements improvements would be made. The British, in contrast, built both mills and railroads for the ages.

Between 1834 and 1854 railroads helped to expand the markets of northeastern manufactures.[5] Previously goods for the large urban markets had been produced only in the immediate metropolitan area or where rivers or canals provided transportation, and canals themselves generally followed the river valleys. In contrast, railroads could penetrate any area and compete successfully with turnpike or more roundabout canal traffic. Rail not only increased the size of the market but greatly speeded the rate of turnover of inventory. For example, by canal the delivery of coal from Reading to Philadelphia took about four days. By the railroad, from 1839 on, it took only that many hours. New connections could be made to the transmontane West, as when the Philadelphia and Columbia, the first trunkline, spanned the eighty miles between the inland Pennsylvania river and canal system and the port of Philadelphia in 1834. Rail also made possible better connections between major manufacturing areas, as when, in 1841, three connecting roads from Boston reached East Albany, New York.[6]

But the economic effect of the railroad was not dramatic. It was a "slow, continual, creeping improvement in rail transport," writes Paul H. Cootner, "that improved its competitive position." The greatest aid to railroads came from "steady reduction in the costs of iron machinery . . . rather than because of major technological advances."[7] Although the 1830s was a decade of more railroad building in the United States than in Britain, only at its end were Baltimore, Philadelphia, and New York connected by rail, and one had to wait another decade to go by train from Boston to Washington or from New York City up the Hudson River. Consequently, except perhaps for the immediate Boston and Philadelphia areas, the effects of railroads in this first decade of building were greater in the demand for equipment than in reorganizing the shipment of goods.

Railroad construction required initial capital investments far larger than any previously made in private corporations. These sums were raised by individual subscriptions to stock supplemented by funds from state, county, and local governments, which were raised by selling their own bonds, as they had done previously to finance canals and turn-pikes. Requirements for private capital were further eased by paying for construction and equipment chiefly in the securities of the road. Starting in the 1820s, when common stock was the usual means of corporate finance, railroad fund raisers quickly innovated most of the modern forms of securities. Preferred stock soon supplemented common stock. Then came first mortgage bonds administered by a trustee, such as Girard Trust of Philadelphia as early as 1839. And finally, in the 1840s and 1850s there were equipment trust bonds and debenture bonds that offered the holder the security of a lien on certain goods or of ranking ahead of stock in case of corporate reorganization in bankruptcy. In time all of these new forms of securities were to be used by other types of corporations, but in the early days manufacturing enterprises could not expect to finance by bonds other than those secured by real estate and buildings.[8]

Payment for construction in the securities of the road, particularly in common stock before there was much improved property to mortgage, would frequently end in the construction company becoming the chief stockholder. Therefore, the promoters of the railroad, for their own protection, were usually large participants in the rather unrelated activity of construction. Since up to about 1847 it was hard to raise large sums of money by public financing, all but a very few roads tended to have a top-heavy financial structure, with very large annual interest payments owed to the public and private bondholders. The hopes of insiders for profit, therefore, had to be more in selling supplies, land, bridges, and equipment to the railroad than in expecting large dividends and rapidly rising prices for the company stock.

Building in both directions, between 1849 and 1854 railroads connected the Northeast Coast with Chicago and the Mississippi Valley. When the Pennsylvania reached Pittsburgh in 1852, the Pittsburgh and Fort Wayne took traffic on west. A year later, when the York Central was consolidated to Buffalo, the Lake Shore and Michigan Southern already continued along the south shore of Lake Erie and eventually to Chicago. Similarly, when the Baltimore and Ohio reached the river at Wheeling, late in the year 1853, a connecting road led on into Ohio.

These early connections were chiefly valuable for passengers and fast freight; bulky goods traveled far more cheaply by water. In the previous decades, what was now the Middle West had developed a high degree of self-sufficiency in iron, wood, and leather working, food processing, and textiles. While 1853–54 saw the beginning of a more closely knit national market extending beyond the Mississippi River, gaining a secure position in this widespread market was a slow and costly process for north-eastern firms, one which required larger capital and new methods of selling.

Another change in business practices, almost as important as those caused by the railroad, was brought about by the telegraph. It could reduce to a few minutes the time needed to transmit an order over hundreds of miles, thereby nearly halving the time consumed in the marketing of manufactured goods and giving companies far better control over their sales agents. In 1837 Samuel F. B. Morse, a professor of fine art at New York University, had made the system commercially practical by perfecting transmission and reception in code, but both government and business were slow at first in adopting this major innovation. By 1850, however, adoption was rapid, and as early as 1851 several railroads were controlling operations by telegraph. The general market for telegraph equipment continued to be shared by many non-connecting and unreliable competitors. Only in America was telegraph strictly a private enterprise.[9]

II

Railroads suddenly created a demand for items seldom or never made before. Locomotives, cast iron car wheels, trucks and frames, rails and bridges were needed in quantity. The largest part of the new business in iron centered in the Philadelphia-Wilmington area, but parts of local railroad demand were met in the New York City area and other manufacturing centers all over the nation. Glenn Porter and Harold C. Livesay note that "never before had so few customers demanded so much material," and, it might be added, from a large number of potential suppliers.[10] By the 1840s railroads accounted for about one-third of total industrial demand for iron.[11] Locomotives were always specially ordered items, and such work might be done in small shops as well as in large. Up to 1842 Porter and Livesay see this demand being largely met by direct negotiation with producers, the latter usually having to take much of their pay in railroad securities. From then on, as orders became still larger, they were placed with commission merchants who divided them among suppliers and assumed part, at least, of the risk of granting credit.

The earliest roads were built with flat rails about 5/8 inch thick and 2

1/2 inches wide, spiked on the top of wooden stringers about 6 inches square. Such rails were generally supplied from domestic mills. A congressional act of July 1832 that exempted iron actually laid on railroads or inclined planes from tariff duty opened the door to coke-smelted British T or H rails, which could not be produced as cheaply in the United States. Parts of the Pennsylvania Mainline and of other through roads completed between 1832 and 1844 had British rails, although mining roads and local branches, as well as sections of road completed before 1832, continued to use domestic flat rails. The Albany and Schenectady on the main New York line west, for example, did not convert to T rails until 1850, and even then only under pressure of a state law of 1844. Meanwhile a number of serious accidents occurred from flat rails coming loose and as "snakeheads" penetrating cars or derailing trains.[12]

While the railroad's demand for iron was spectacular in novelty and in concentration of orders, the main volume of domestic iron production was still in castings for ships, supports for buildings, blacksmith work, guns, and most of all for stoves. For all the large-scale uses of wrought and sheet iron, the new anthracite smelting with a hot blast, available after 1840, was cheaper and as satisfactory as the traditional charcoal product. The new method grew with railroad and other demands for cheap iron until by 1854, when the American Iron Association started collecting statistics, anthracite was used to smelt 45 percent of the domestic pig iron.[13] But in 1855 the British Committee on the Machinery of the United States claimed that charcoal smelting made American cast iron, as well as nails, superior to iron produced with anthracite or coke.[14] Until the advent of cheap steel, smiths also preferred the more familiar and malleable charcoal-smelted iron for tools, guns, and other fine work.

With a specific duty of $25 a ton placed on railroad iron by the tariff of 1842, there seemed to be a chance for rails rolled domestically to compete with those from Britain. As a result, late in 1844 the first U rails, a variant type of all-iron rail soon abandoned in the United States, were rolled from coke-smelted iron at the Mt. Savage works in Maryland for the nearby Baltimore and Ohio Railroad.[15] A few months later the Montour Iron Works bought pig from the Danville branch of the Phoenix Company of Pennsylvania and rolled the first T rails from anthracite smelted pig.

The market soon collapsed. In 1846 tariff protection was reduced to 30 percent ad valorem, and the British iron industry, hit by the end of a domestic railroad boom and a general depression, flooded the market at cut rates. By 1850, of the fifteen or sixteen United States mills that had been equipped for rolling rails, only two were in production.[16] Increasing demand in the great American railroad boom from 1849 to 1854 and Britain's entry into the Crimean War brought the American rail mills back to life, and rerolling old rails aided rapid growth.

III

As with most of the other producers in early industrialization, the iron industry remained in the hands of the separate proprietors of numerous furnaces, forges, and rolling mills, chiefly in Pennsylvania. Only the Colemans' furnaces at Cornwall were really large scale, smelting local ore with charcoal from the family's extensive holding of nearby timber. Members of the Coleman family invested in surrounding forges, but no tight integration was attempted. Furnace owners usually sold to iron merchants in the port cities, who in turn directed the iron to processors and ultimately to consumers. Fully integrated iron or steel production came only after 1855.

The chief changes before 1850 were in adapting new technology to Middle States coal and ores. Before the late 1830s Pennsylvania anthracite, which was to become increasingly important to mid-century industrialization, had been used only for heating, and western bituminous coal could not sell east of the mountains. The city gas lighting plants that had started with Baltimore in 1816 had been run on bituminous coal from England, Virginia, or Nova Scotia. The upswing in the use of anthracite for both industrial and home heating started in 1831. Its use as a smelting and refining fuel in the 1840s increased the concentration of iron and coal production in eastern Pennsylvania and made coal the chief export from Philadelphia. yet even though charcoal smelting was not cheaper than smelting with anthracite, the product was often preferred by buyers.[17]

There were no large deposits of good coking coal east of the Alleghenies. By 1850 three northeastern furnaces were using coke, but the quality of iron produced was poor and apparently its lower selling price canceled the saving in the cost of coke as against anthracite.[18] Meanwhile a large deposit of high quality coking coal had been opened at Connellsville south of Pittsburgh. In 1853 this deposit was tapped for making rails on a large scale by the Cambria Iron Company at Johnstown, about midway between Pittsburgh and the Susquehanna River.

Use of coke in the Pittsburgh area waited, however, for a brief revival in the western demand for railroad iron in 1860.

To summarize a situation confusing to ironmasters as well as to buyers and historians: pig iron smelted with anthracite, charcoal, or coke had varying qualities, depending in the case of bituminous coke very much on the character of the coal; buyers needed widely different qualities in iron, which came in part from the fuel used for smelting the ore; smelters were generally independent of processors; rolling mills produced 50 percent more product for the capital invested than forges with half the labor cost; and finally, no scientists, in the United States at least, understood the chemistry behind many of the differences in quality. This last factor inevitably led ironmasters to rely on experience and to fear experimentation.

The greater geographical concentration of the British industry no doubt facilitated the spread of new knowledge, whereas in America even most of the Maryland and Pennsylvania works were too far apart for easy consultation. The differences between the two nations appear, however, to have been more the product of the character and location of natural resources and of the size of different types of demand than of technical know-how. Eastern Pennsylvania ores were more siliceous than those of Britain and required up to twice as much limestone for satisfactory smelting with anthracite, making the American process seem inefficient by comparison. There was a little more knowledge of iron metallurgy in England, although probably nothing important that had not been read about in the United States. In the 1850s a leading British engineer wrote, "The American machinist takes every opportunity of becoming acquainted with our inventions and scientific literature."[19] The reverse was not true. The British of mid-century were likely to be unaware of American advances. But not all new processes were written up for some time after their initial development. During this same decade William Kelley in Kentucky and Henry Bessemer in England developed and patented processes for making steel cheaply. Bessemer, however, was helped to commercial success by two nearby chemists, whereas Kelley, working alone at Cambria Iron Company, failed to achieve reliably profitable production.[20]

An increasing demand for iron in ships reinforced the needs of railroads and was often supplied from the same shops. The first successful boats to be made entirely from iron were canal barges finished in

1829 for eastern Pennsylvania coal shipments, which by 1840 were part of the most important domestic interregional trade. Iron barges were lighter weight in relation to carrying capacity than wooden barges, and in the heartland of the iron industry only slightly more expensive. Much of this building of barges for use on inland waterways went on in Pittsburgh, almost invariably in firms that also made boilers.[21]

Britain, spurred by its shortage of wood, had been building iron boats for all purposes, including offshore routes, since around 1820. In the 1820s British iron parts were sent to the United States for assembly. The fact that small iron vessels could not safely navigate the North Atlantic, however, gave American iron, and shipyards, a degree of protection, and also enabled shipbuilders to supply the Central American market for iron river boats by delivery under their own steam. In the 1840s small iron boats, both propeller and sidewheel, were being built in all the northeastern shipbuilding centers and also at Pittsburgh. The largest amount of tonnage of all types originated in the New York City area, but the shipyards there concentrated mainly on wooden sailing ships for offshore and overseas trade. The boiler and engine makers from Philadelphia to Wilmington, the second largest shipbuilding area, became the pioneers in iron screw propeller boats and in 1845 were producing ships of over four hundred gross tons. These soon became important in the coastal trade, and by 1850 they had crossed the Atlantic.[22]

Propeller-driven ships had to be of iron, as the shafts loosened wooden frames. Most of these ships were of narrow beam and shallow draft for use on rivers and canals. Twin screws were adopted early in order to lessen draft and reduce turbulence along the canal banks. In 1844 George H. Aspinwall of New York ordered two small twin screw boats built in Philadelphia to run between there and Troy, New York, by way of the Delaware and Raritan Canal. They demonstrated seaworthiness by sailing to New York City via the Atlantic and were ultimately bought by the government for transport during the war with Mexico. By 1842 there was a line of iron steamers operating between Philadelphia and Hartford, Connecticut.[23]

Iron ships for the immense coal trade were not generally steam-powered. Anthracite had become the most desirable heating fuel by 1830, and northeastern Pennsylvania was practically its only source. Coal for shipment from Philadelphia was brought to dockside by iron barges of up to 180 tons capacity, as well as by the Reading Railroad. At dozens of wharves it was transferred to sailing schooners of both wood and iron bound up and down the coast. Anthracite also reached New York City through the Delaware and Hudson Canal.

Anthracite burned with a heat so intense that it destroyed iron boilers, and its use by railroads was delayed. Coal-carrying railroads burned wood in their locomotives until 1852, when James Millholand of the Reading perfected a boiler that would stand the heat produced by anthracite. But since anthracite mines were limited to a small area and bituminous coal deposits were widely distributed over Pennsylvania, Virgina, Kentucky, and the Middle West, it was bituminous coal that gradually supplanted wood as the fuel for most railroads.

IV

The 1840s and 1850s were a period when the spread of transportation to new centers in the Middle West brought them into a national market. In the Northeast, however, it was also a period of increasingly high productivity from an already well-established industrial system. Never before or since in United States history has value added by manufacture increased at as rapid a rate as between the census data collected in 1839 and 1849, with most of the increase undoubtedly coming after 1842 and continuing at a high rate until 1855.

The big textile mills of northeastern Massachusetts remained the largest factories, turning out cheap cloth for the domestic, Latin American, and Far Eastern markets. They were said by an English observer, James Montgomery, to turn out more yarn and cloth per spindle than any in the world, and to use less labor per automatic loom.[24] As business boomed from 1843 to 1846, American cheap cottons continued to be competitive with the British in world markets. By 1850 Massachusetts and Rhode Island had nearly half the cotton spindles of the United States. The type of mill varied greatly between the two states. In contrast to the gigantic mills of Boston-controlled corporations at Lawrence and Lowell, each with over a thousand employees, the average enterprise in Rhode Island was small and unincorporated. Instead of the integration of the Massachusetts industry, dying, bleaching, and printing were done in Providence by separate companies, a demonstration that in the textile industry in the United States, as in England, the economies of scale from the integration of processes was limited.[25] Meanwhile Philadelphia maintained its lead in fine cottons, plus their printing in designs such as calicoes, and also in woolen goods, including carpets. More than two-thirds of the spindles in Pennsylvania were within thirty miles of Philadelphia, producing a concentration similar to those of Rhode Island and northeastern Massachusetts. In 1846 William Gregg of Charleston, South Carolina, built a large textile mill at nearby Granitesville, but in general textiles remained a northeastern industry.[26]

Because of abundant waterpower in the Northeast, American master mechanics had by 1800 taken the lead in solving practical problems in hydraulics. Unlike French engineers, the Americans were not highly educated. They did not write articles for encyclopedias or present theoretical papers. Consequently, while American use of new devices came as early and on a greater scale than in France, it is the French engineers who have appeared in history texts. As a result of experiments from the late 1820s on by Benoit Fourneyron, Feu Jonval, and others in France, and chiefly by Austin and Zebulon Parker and Samuel B. Howd in America, a fan type of enclosed wheel was developed, called a turbine. Turbines began to replace existing wheels In the Lowell and Philadelphia areas in 1842. The turbine could double efficneicy, but it was expensive to build, install, and repair, and to be economical it needed to run at full capacity. Hence in both France and America use of the turbine spread slowly.[27]

In spite of successful installations of water turbines, from the 1840s on country mills on streams joined those of the big cities in turning to the more costly but reliable steampower. John Leander Bishop estimated that in 1836 less than 1 percent of American cotton spindles were turned by steam, but in textile machinery as a whole, and in other metalworking industries, the percentage using steam was already high by 1840.[28] In Alfred Jenks's pioneer textile machinery mill at Bridesburg in Philadelphia County, for example, iron was moved around a four-acre plant by rail, lifted by steam, and shaped by steam-driven machinery. By mid-century the works employed about four hundred men and sold nationally through illustrated catalogs.[29] From an early day the Providence machinery industry was also dependent on steam. Since in Massachusetts the machine work was generally located on streams near the mills, waterpower lasted longer.

By mid-century, leadership in the wide variety of light industries of different types was divided between Britain and the northeastern United States. Connecticut led both at home and abroad in mass-produced firearms and led the United States in cutlery and brass working, although the metal for the latter came from New York City and Philadelphia. In Massachusetts and some other states plants were said to draw wire more cheaply than in Britain.[30] Henry Disston's factory for making saws in Philadelphia claimed in 1850 to be the largest in the world.[31] In heavy metalwork the Philadelphia-Wilmington area remained the largest source of products, with metropolitan New York City and Pittsburgh second and third.[32]

Looking at the Northeast as a whole, from the late 1830s to 1850 the greatest development in both agriculture and industry was in the state of New York. Both New York and Pennsylvania grew extremely rapidly, but by 1850 New York State led in most farm products, including animals, and in the total value of manufactures. In fact, state manufacturing output was about equal in value to that of agriculture.[33] Meanwhile, because of sugar refining and finished clothing, New York City forged slightly ahead of Philadelphia in value of product, but not in capital invested in manufacturing. In fact, the coal, iron, and clothing businesses were so intertwined between the two areas, and with the intervening cities of Paterson and Trenton, that it is more realistic to think of one great manufacturing complex from Wilmington to New York.[34] From 1843 to 1860 this megalopolis was probably the most rapidly growing large industrial area in the world.

In addition to these industries that lay at the base of industrial strength, the use of machinery was continually applied to older products. Flour milling was so fully mechanized that little more could be added, but leather and wood working used increasing numbers of machines. Paints, chemicals, and pharmaceuticals, for which Philadelphia was the center, achieved ever more mechanization and economies of scale. In the middle 1840s papermaking and printing benefited from the rotary press invented by the American Richard Hoe. By the next decade the sewing machine, first perfected in the United States by Elias Howe, was greatly reducing the cost of any goods that needed fine stitching and boosting the output of ready-made clothing, a particularly American product. This continual improvement and increase in the use of machinery was still a product of American cultural drives and interests, or as Paul Uselding puts it, "the result of deliberative and purposeful managerial behavior. . . . The labor scarcity hypothesis is not a sufficient explanation for the observed, dominant labor saving efficiency growth in the period 1841–1850."[35]

Between 1840 and 1860 agricultural machinery production became increasingly important. Winnowing and threshing for wheat reached a plateau of mechanization by 1840 that was not substantially exceeded for some decades. The McCormick reaper, also for wheat, was put into large-scale production at a plant in Chicago in 1848 and began to sell widely on the level prairie farms. The 1840s and 1850s saw myriad new mechanical devices to ease and speed farm cultivation, but relatively few farmers bought the newest products in either machinery or fertilizers. In 1860 the value of machinery per improved farm acre stood at $2.14 in Pennsylvania, $2.03 in New York, $1.80 in Massachusetts, and only $1.38 in Ohio.[36]

The manufacturing sector of the economy grew substantially between 1849 and 1859, but not at the rate of the previous decade. As noted earlier, the years of most rapid growth, 1845–54, overlap the census periods. The percentage of the labor force listed by the census as engaged in manufacturing remained at 12.5 percent in the census of 1860, but increased in absolute figures by over 350,000, and value added by manufacture nearly doubled. The New York–Brooklyn area produced the largest value of manufactured product in both 1850 and 1860, with Philadelphia second, although the latter at both dates employed more people and claimed a larger capital invested. These two leading industrial centers produced substantially more than all the states to the westward, north of Tennessee, and twice the value of the products of all the southern states.

V

While the United States of 1850, because of its continental extent, was still agricultural as measured by either employment or production, its Northeast had gone through the first and critical phases of industrialization. Along with the advanced nations of Western Europe, the northeastern United States was on the frontier of technological change, and, in spite of occasional leads or lags, all leading nations would advance substantially together. From the start in the 1780s there had been a tendency for America to draw experimental ideas from Europe and then put them to practical, commercial use, and this process continued during the middle and later nineteenth century. Since the larger share of the improvement in new processes usually came from manufacture and use, it can be contended that the United States was practically the world leader in efficient methods of mass fabrication.

As if to celebrate this maturity, the Crystal Palace Exposition in London in 1851 attracted worldwide attention to American machines and a number of their products. The British government, fearful that Britain was losing leadership in some areas of armament, sent a Committee on Machinery of the United States to America to investigate "the American System" of mass production.[37] Its report was published in 1855 as *The American System of Manufactures*. Shaking the complacency of many British proprietors of metalworks, the report showed that machinery was more heavily utilized in America, at a large saving in cost. The same was true of many areas of manufacture other than metals. In woodworking, for example, American plants were almost completely mechanized. That such plants used wood more wastefully than did British handworkers illustrates a general lavishness with cheap raw materials in many types of fabrication by machines. As John E. Sawyer has observed, "These early American innovators often seem to have more clearly seen the general principles and potentialities of their departures from traditional ways than their contemporaries elsewhere. . . . The basic features of all this were being illustrated by the mid-century."[38]

The British observers also concluded that in the United States workshop room was better apportioned to work, partly because of better plant organization; that the workers were well disciplined; and that more special machines were used than in Britain. Although the observers devoted much of their time to plants manufacturing ordnance, it seems reasonable to conclude that American production, as a whole, was the most mechanized in the world and that the British period of world leadership in machinery had really ended sometime earlier.[39]

The spread of railroads and some additional canals had not only given the United States a national market for products; it also opened nationwide sources of raw materials. From precious metals in the Sierras and Rockies, to lumber from Wisconsin, copper and iron from Michigan, coal from Missouri and the Ohio Valley, and food from the Middle West, there were supplies that to the men of mid-century seemed inexhaustible. Transportation costs were high, but initial production costs were low, and the increased use of machinery at all stages was thought to be the avenue for becoming competitive in world markets. This did not happen overnight. In some cases, such as in iron and steel production, the lower wages and costs of transportation in Europe were not overcome by American machinery in worldwide sales until the late 1880s. In food products, European tariffs and regulations checked American exports. But at home, tariff protection increasingly reduced imports to specialties and luxury goods.

In finance, trade, and service, the United States had no ascendancy over Old World practices. State jealousies and divisions had weakened banking after 1835; American trading and shipowning houses were putting their capital into more profitable internal development. Yet at the end of the great railroad boom in 1854, during which the United States was annually laying as much track as all of Europe, this "young" nation was the world leader in many types of machine equipment. It was also said to have more children per capita in school than any country save Denmark, a good portent for further economic growth.

7

The Evolving Business System

Improvements in business practices and growth in the size of markets were mutually reinforcing. Starting about 1790 and continuing in the nineteenth century, cities of over eight thousand inhabitants in general, and the major northeastern ports in particular, grew rapidly, the latter containing a total of over one million people by 1840. Growth came not only from immigration, both domestic and foreign, but also from increasing managerial and technological efficiency in trade with the hinterland, which brought in food, fuel, and raw materials at low prices in return for city-made products. As urban centers grew on a self-sufficient basis from the production and trade of the local area, city dwellers gradually became their own best customers.[1] Intercity trade also grew, but up to 1840 at slower rates. For example, Philadelphians burned anthracite in grates made in Troy, and steamboats made on the Delaware served on the Hudson, but large increases in volume of intercity trade awaited increasing specialization in the manufacturing of each area, as well as uninterrupted canal or rail connections.

I

A larger volume of business increased mercantile specialization and created new occupations. "Drummers" working on commission waited on the wharves and at coach stations and hotel lobbies to persuade out-of-town buyers to visit certain local merchants. But jobbers in touch with backcountry storekeepers might already have tied up the prospective buyer through advance correspondence. In the largest metropolitan markets importers and wholesalers could specialize in certain products, as the Browns of Baltimore did in Irish linens, and by steady patronage of suppliers they could arrange for prices and variety that might undercut both the auction markets and the old-style general importer.[2] The early 1830s especially, were a profitable period for expanding specialized firms, like the Browns, which soon had branches in Philadelphia and New York.

Particularly after the expiration of the federal charter of the Second Bank of the United States, these big mercantile firms could also do a profitable business in foreign and domestic exchange between the ports, thus paving the way for some merchants to move completely into investment banking. Their success in investment banking underscores the control of the market exercised by mercantile credit. Many inland buyers were tied to certain merchants by advances of goods or cash. Much of the export trade in raw materials was financed by the houses of the port cities, and these firms preferred to sell imported rather than domestic goods to the backcountry.

By 1840 the specialized importing companies were operating efficiently enough to supersede the auctioneers in disposing of large shipments of imports, and the auction system gradually died out. It should be emphasized that while these new means of marketing and shipping were products of denser population and higher income, they, in turn, contributed to the rise in per capita income that increased the demand for industrial products. Some products, such as chemicals and pharmaceuticals, were scarcely ever made in the hinterland, and urban producers and jobbers had a large trade with even the remote backcountry.

II

To increased and faster communication between the coastal cities, especially by scheduled packet lines, there were added new regional business services. National credit rating was needed because inland sales were ordinarily on a six-month basis for payment and might require extension of notes for as much as a year longer. In the 1820s drug firms in Philadelphia and dry goods jobbers in New York City commissioned southern and western credit investigators, and in some trades the large companies exchanged credit information. In 1829 the London banking house of Baring Brothers commissioned Thomas Wren Ward of Boston to provide them regularly with credit information on American businessmen. An effective rating system developed, which was used by Barings for thirty years. A New York City firm—Griffen, Cleveland and Campbell—used country lawyers to report on the credit of merchants in their area and in 1835 spread the ratings to parts of Pennsylvania. In return the local lawyer was given the business of collection from delinquents. The firm claimed to have over one hundred clients. apparently this pioneer venture failed to grow during the depression years after 1837, and the accounts were acquired by Lewis Tappan, a neighbor in lower Manhattan, who opened his own "mercantile Agency" in 1841. As Tappan succeeded by the same means employed by Griffen, Cleveland and Campbell, additional agencies entered the field. By 1850 nationwide credit rating had become an established service.[3]

The businesslike character of the six-cent daily papers had delayed the start of a specialized commercial press. The dailies, read chiefly by businessmen and politicians, carried "Prices Current," shipping news, and many columns of trade advertising. There was also *Niles' Weekly Register*, published in Baltimore, which included some commercial as well as political news. A first step toward greater specialization was the *New York General Shipping and Commercial List*, a semiweekly started in 1815 and continuing under different names throughout the century. But until 1827 no other big city publisher successfully launched a special business paper.[4] In none of these activities were European nations markedly ahead of the United States.

By the end of the 1820s cities, with approximately 11 percent of all households in the United States, were large enough, printing sufficiently improved, and paper cheap enough to bring about two connected developments: the popularly read one-cent daily and periodicals devoted to business. The first attempt at a penny daily in Philadelphia failed in 1830, but the New York *Sun*, started in 1833, succeeded and was soon copied in the other major cities. Penny papers, written for a wide public, lacked the business news of the six-cent dailies. If a businessman were to purchase a second periodical he might be tempted by a specialized publication. *The New York Journal of Commerce* (1827–) and Samuel Hazard's *Register of Pennsylvania* (1828–36) were given over chiefly to statistics regarding business in the state and nation. In 1831 D. K. Minor and Henry V. Poor started *The American Railroad Journal* in New York. But the most famous general periodical, Freeman Hunt's *Merchant's Magazine and Commercial Review*, did not appear in New York until 1839. In 1846 a *Bankers Magazine and State Financial Register* added to the general business literature.[5] The same developments went on to a lesser degree in England at about the same dates.[6]

The reinforcement to developing industrial business provided by the business press must have been moderate in total effect. Perhaps more important was the contemporaneous development of technological societies and their periodicals. They were an outgrowth of a movement extending over all the large northeastern cities, as far west as Cincinnati, for the establishment of special libraries and institutes for mechanics. The earliest reading room was the Apprentice's Library in Philadelphia in 1819, followed the next year by two in Boston. The first Mechanical and Scientific Institute was formed in New York City in 1822, a year before a similar organization in London, but the most famous early society was the Franklin Institute, started in Philadelphia in 1824. It was a direct outgrowth of the advanced metalworking industry of this leading manufacturing center. Its chief subscribers and directors, such as Mathias Baldwin, Franklin Peale, and James Sellers, were actively engaged in businesses prospering from mechanical improvements. Bruce Sinclair has explained that "the central and chief concern of the Franklin Institute exhibitions from 1824 to 1838 was to advance the technical level of manufacturing skills, to increase the use of mechanical power, and to develop mineral resources."[7] From 1826 on the institute published the *Franklin Journal and American Mechanics Magazine* (after 1828, *Journal of the Franklin Institute*), edited by Thomas P. Jones, who had started the *Mechanics' Magazine* in New York the year before.[8] Baltimore established a similar type of institute in 1826, and Boston in 1827.

The periodicals of the technological societies were undoubtedly read by employers and scientists rather than by workers. An effort at blending science and technology in a mechanics' school at the Franklin Institute failed to attract students. The chief role of the periodicals was to make available the new developments in the nation and abroad to those capable of understanding and applying them. Yet for two more decades, at least, most practical engineers preferred to travel to where the new invention was being used and study it in operation. George Sellers of Philadelphia thought that the several hundred master mechanics of the English-speaking world knew of each other by name and reputation. Travel and observation were encouraged by the fact that some very able practical mechanics were unable to read and translate small-scale plans into workable machinery.[9]

In these innovative years of the 1820s engineering education was also formalized in the United States. From its founding in 1802, the Military Academy at West Point had given its graduates general training in military engineering, but no other school had such courses. In 1824 Stephen Van Rensselaer founded the Rensselaer Polytechnic Institute at Troy, New York, to "instruct the sons and daughters of farmers and mechanics . . . [in] the application of science to the common purposes of life."[10] Started with a strong interest in chemistry, the school soon switched its emphasis to civil engineering as a result of the railroad boom. No other engineering, as distinct from scientific, schools appeared before mid-century. Partly because of the immigration of European engineers such as Prussian-trained J. A. Roebling, and partly because machines were still at a stage where little scientific, as opposed to technical, knowledge was needed, lack of engineering education equivalent to that available in France or Germany did not appear to impede industrialization in the United States.

Technical education for business leaders came through meetings in societies and associations. Philadelphia, a center of interest in both inland transportation and manufacturing, was the home of numerous such societies. In addition to older ones for industry and agriculture, a Pennsylvania Society for the Promotion of Internal Improvements was formed in January 1825, which promptly sent William Strickland to England to study railroads. He brought home a working model of a Stephenson locomotive, and his *Reports on Canals, Railways, Roads and Other Subjects* was published the following year.[11] Fortunately his recommendations for the British practice of sleepers of stone and rails of cast iron were not adopted by major American railroads. A Philadelphia board of trade was founded in 1834, the year the Mainline to Pittsburgh was completed. Similar organizations continually appeared in all the major cities. General merchants' exchanges rapidly followed the New York model of 1827. In all types of societies businessmen learned of new technology, new trade and financial practices, and opportunities for new ventures. Being, as Alexis de Tocqueville put it, "a nation of joiners" was a strong aid to American economic advance.

III

The support of governments and the favorable interpretation of the laws by the courts continued to stimulate business action. Incorporation, already easy compared to other nations, was further facilitated by state legislatures adopting general acts. The principle of such an act specifying a uniform charter to which companies subscribed by simple application to a state officer had been established in New Jersey, New York, and Pennsylvania before 1800 for certain types of nonprofit organizations. Massachusetts in 1809 and New York two years later led the way in passing general acts for mnaufacturing corporations. These early acts were designed to encourage incorporation by making it simpler and cheaper than lobbying through a special act. After many corporate failures in the late 1830s and early 1840s, general acts became reform measures to prevent companies from gaining special privileges through obscure clauses never understood by many of the legislators who voted for them. In the twenty years after 1838 Massachusetts, New Jersey, New York, Pennsylvania, and Virginia passed general acts for all types of nonfinancial business corporations. Originally these "reform" charters were not compulsory and the incorporators might introduce a special legislative act, but between 1850 and 1880 almost all the leading industrial states passed laws prohibiting special charters.[12] Surveying the history as a whole, however, incorporation in the United States remained easier and more open to special provisions than elsewhere. In Britain incorporation was simplified only in the 1840s, and in France and Germany not until the 1860s.[13]

The federal system, in practice, gave greater freedom to corporations than the centralized systems of Europe. After the United States Supreme Court in the *Dartmouth College* case (1820) ruled that corporate charters were contracts protected by the Constitution from revision, corporate activity became difficult to regulate adversely. In the 1820s state courts upheld limited liability for stockholders in case of bankruptcy. In the next decade states granted railroad corporations the right of eminent domain. The ruling in *Bank of Augusta v. Earle* (1839)—that in the absence of any law to the contrary a corporation could do business in any state—may have seemed inevitable, but the Supreme Court had to reverse a contrary decision by the circuit court. The states acting under police or public welfare doctrines were supported by the courts in a few cases, but in general corporations continued to live a relatively free life.[14]

Relations between business leaders and the state governments varied, but most legislatures remained anxious to promote economic development. Large state debts and the depression of 1839 to 1843, however, temporarily cooled legislative ardor for subsidies or loans. In the leading industrial states of New York and Pennsylvania, and particularly in the latter, there was strong backcountry opposition to corporations. The result was that the supporters of internal development often had to buy backcountry votes for state-financed improvements by including uneconomical projects in the distant rural areas. In the case of Pennsylvania this amounted to a considerable diversion of capital to unnecessary construction and maintenance of canals.

The tariff was probably a stimulant to the growth of local enterprise, but this has been argued both ways. There is merit in the classic argument that investment in industries that could only survive with protection took capital away from activities that for one reason or another did not have to fear foreign competition. Light and regressive taxation at both state and federal levels assisted entrepreneurs in mobilizing financial resources.

IV

A "factory," defined as a plant administered by at least one salaried supervisor, as distinct from a "shop" managed wholly by the proprietor, involved new types of skills in handling both machines and workers. The general picture that emerges in the period before about 1830 is of large variations in both worker and managerial achievement. Joseph Stancliffe Davis believed that poor management went far to explain the failures among early manufacturing companies.[15] Men, women, and children coming from farm life to large, impersonal factories with several hundred workers had to learn to report for work on time and regularly. In the case of unskilled workers, including most all the women and children in the work force, "industrial discipline" could be maintained by threat of firing. But in skilled work, as in the metal industries, workers might recognize the difficulty of replacing them and act accordingly. In such situations the personality of the foreman or supervisor could be very important. Knowledge and ability also commanded respect from workers. The boss who could do anyone's job was listened to.

The structure of plant management varied greatly between industries. In a machine shop with over two hundred workers, such as Sellers and Pennock in Philadelphia, the man responsible for each type of operation was simply the number-one workman, and the partners supervised the operation as a whole.[16] In an equally large textile mill there were recognized positions of responsibility: carder, spinning room overseer, throstle room overseer, boss weaver, and overseer of looms, as well as a general supervisor. These lower managers received much higher pay than the operatives and might earn bonuses for productivity in their departments.[17]

Managerial abilities of all types were enhanced by the interchanges in ideas that went on in city environments. While plants using water-power, as well as canals and railroads, were necessarily spread over the countryside, their controlling proprietors or investors usually lived in the major cities. As steam displaced waterpower, particularly in small-scale uses of power and in metal manufacturing, cities grew still more as manufacturing centers.

Beyond plant management lay new problems in coordination of supply and demand, of having a product reliable in both quantity and quality, and the means of reaching the best jobbers and wholesalers. Old-style merchants took on these new functions. As with the Boston group that financed the cotton textile factory at Waltham in 1814, merchants frequently supplied all or most of the initial capital for an industrial venture and then took over the marketing of the product. Industry, as such, was probably a net debtor up to 1850.[18] In cases of mercantile finance and control the plant supervisors would take orders from a mill agent, who was subordinate to the suppliers of funds. Such complete control by the marketers seems to have been more common in textiles than in metalworking. Here merchants might coordinate the movement of iron from ore to bars ready for manufacture, but the plants such as those of the Sellers, Baldwin, or Norris in Philadelphia were financially independent of their agents.

V

The major change, or revolution, in management—the rise of special-ized bureaucratic control in large companies—was to grow rapidly only after 1850, but the directions of this change had become clear by the 1820s. Managerial enterprise, or control by officers who own relatively little stock in the company, had begun with the first banks, 1781–84, and had necessarily been the rule in insurance, turnpike, canal, and large coal and navigation companies. On the basis of a "critical point" analysis—emphasis on the time when a trend was not to be reversed— this form of control was securely established for certain types of en-terprises in the early nineteenth century. But just as Evans's or Fulton's works were not typical of general iron processing, these large firms represented a departure from the usual historic forms of control of small enterprise by proprietors.

On any turnpike fifty miles long it was impossible for a general manager personally to oversee toll collections and maintenance. Authority had to be delegated to one or more divisional superintendents. The basic management problem of proper delegation of authority and degrees of head office control became still more pressing on the longer canals. Railroads introduced new problems. The turnpike or canal superintendents had only to be responsible for the road or waterway, whereas on railroads local men remote from the head office had to operate and repair the rolling stock as well as run freight and ticket offices.

By the 1840s expansion of railroad companies to 150 or more miles of first-line track and of mining companies to operations of several types at distant locations introduced the problems of the modern large corporation. Uneven layers of middle management had to be coordinated, and managers had to be selected or promoted because of their expertise or ability rather than their share in ownership. Such problems afflicted companies like Lehigh Coal and Navigation, which owned mines, railroads, canals, and distributing centers and which had by 1840 over two thousand employees of many different types. Their variety produced management problems different and far more complex than would two thousand workers in adjacent textile mills.[19]

While American culture had proven unusually well suited to the management of small- to medium-sized proprietary ventures and to innovations in methods, the culture lacked a place for nonowning managers who could not be directly motivated by personal profits. Americans had not been led to cultivate a zeal for rising in rank and salary by doing a good job; there were no traditions, and few examples, of efficient government or private bureaucracy. Businessmen accustomed to working for personal gains in the market were not used to, or satisfied with, being careerists in hierarchies; they did not easily adjust to passing on orders from above impersonally or to understanding the acceptable roles that went with different statuses. Americans lacked the experience with commitment to duty in large organizations that European feudalism, armies, and governments had instilled in many of their citizens. The cultural interests in tinkering, building, and making money for oneself that served America in other ways had a negative influence in executive suits or in managerial outposts controlled by policies transmitted from the head office.

Consequently the railroad, by increasing the size of enterprises, brought new problems to the United States for which its people were less uniquely qualified than they had been for the problems of the earlier period. The middle managers or skilled workers in stations and shops or on trains often lacked requisite discipline and morale. And as the nation continued to expand rapidly in both population and settled area, a shortage of management for railroads and other far-flung operations became a force limiting economic development. Financier John Murray Forbes of Boston wrote, "While there are a hundred good projects, you will find it hard to choose ten men to manage them."[20] Although some American middle managers were unusually innovative, others lacked sufficient responsibility in carrying out orders. Both traits can be amply documented; the overall balance would have to depend on the type of job and its environment. At mid-century, for example, Charles Francis Adams thought Prussian railroads were better managed than American, whereas the British Committee on the Machinery of the United States had particular praise for the management in the firearms industry.[21]

An economic gain, but an added managerial problem, was the flood of immigrants from 1845 to 1854; probably more arrived in these years than had come in the whole history of the nation up to that time. Immigration, which had varied from 8,000 to 111,000 a year between 1820 and 1845, depending on the state of the European or American economy, jumped to 239,000 by 1847 and to 460,000 by 1854. For the first time since the early days of the colonies the country grew more from the foreign influx than from domestic fertility. Coming very largely from German and Irish farm areas, and financially assisted to leave by their government in the latter case, the newcomers usually lacked both industrial skills and discipline. Their absorption into industry was a challenge to lower management in all large operations.

A solution to the problems of management, widely adopted in the 1840s and 1850s, was "inside contracting." This practice meant breaking an operation down into parts, each of which could be let on a profit-making basis to a small businessman. The leading railroad journalist, Henry V. Poor, suggested that managers might subcontract every part of the operation of the road. The Philadelphia, Wilmington and Baltimore Railroad came as close as was practical to doing just that.

The practice was also widely used in metalworking and mining. But it did not provide a lasting solution. Contracting diminished the ability of central management to hold a market by cutting costs in certain areas or on certain items or to introduce new processes and business structure at a temporary loss. In addition, many subcontractors cut corners and turned out unsatisfactory goods or services that reacted against the reputation of the parent company. Consequently the period from 1840 to the mid-1850s appears to be one in which American business was groping for new forms to fit new problems and turning out to be slow and fumbling in finding them. While the railroad problems were partially met by both experience and a new generation of managers, as late as the 1860s Poor lamented that "railroads . . . will drag along . . . and become worse managed year by year."[22]

The railroad quickly created or emphasized all the complex ethical problems of modern corporate finance. The basic ethical factor was that a partner or proprietor who owned a substantial part of two firms dealing with each other might be on both sides of the buying and selling process without much conflict of interest, whereas the manager who owned half of the selling firm and only one percent of the buying company could clearly make more profit by favoring the seller. Decisions based on self-interest also occurred when renting facilities to a large, publicly owned corporation or to trading in its securities on the basis of inside information. In a culture heavily committed to the virtue of private acquisition, a corporate ethical code developed very slowly. While the dangers were recognized by shrewd observers, such as Nathan Appleton in his book on banking in 1841, protection of small stockholders' interests by top management scarcely began before the 1880s.[23]

During the early decades, however, railroads led the way in several areas: in adopting more elaborate accounting and auditing practices, in separating "staff" functions such as law or engineering from the "line" duties of physical operation, and in delegating authority downward to divisional supervisors. On the frontiers of change, therefore, the railroad appears as the creator of new markets, new business practices, and new managerial structures.

VI

The outlines of the thesis that the business and technological developments that put Americans on the frontiers of industrial change depended on culture, geography, and resources have now been filled in. A business temperament peculiar to the United States colored the process of development a different hue than in Britain or elsewhere in Europe, where conservatism and tradition were stronger. In adjusting to new positions, Americans probably benefited from their habit of moving about and trying new occupations. Although less tradition bound and more willing to face novelty than similar men in Europe, they were not used to hierarchical authority, to being bossed by men they seldom or never saw.

Lured by rapid growth in markets from increases in population, Americans were overoptimistic. There were undoubtedly more business starts per capita and more business failures than elsewhere in the world. While the short average life of enterprises was not in itself favorable to growth, even unsuccessful ventures in new areas were undoubtedly a stimulant to innovation, and, if fixed capital was involved, the buildings, transport facilities, and machines usually remained for a more efficient operator to utilize.

Overoptimism made for more exaggerated up and down swings of the business cycle than in Europe, but it may be that in the long run the intense activity of boom periods generated more in innovative ideas, hard work, and capital investment than the lower activity of the recessions subtracted. At all events, this type of cycle seems to have been inherent in industrial capitalism on new frontiers, where very rapid population growth took place in an area with ample potential resources.

In a long view, the optimistic, competitive temperament of American entrepreneurs seemed best suited to this period of small- to medium-sized firms. Such enterprises have always depended greatly on the practical experience, ability, and drive of the proprietors. Thomas Hamilton, a well-qualified observer from England wrote in 1843, "In that knowledge . . . which the individual acquires for himself by actual observation in ordinary avocations of life, I do not imagine the Americans are excelled by any people in the world."[24] In contrast to the period of early development, when these cultural qualities facilitated rapid economic growth, the period from 1840 on, with its railroads, telegraph, and remote mining operations, required more learning from reading than from observation and more ability to work in structures of authority. Fortunately large enterprise grew slowly and has never become more than a minority segment of business, so that Americans had generations of time to adjust to the more bureaucratic conditions on this frontier of change.

8
Industrial Society

The immense area of the United States, six times that of Western Europe including Britain, has made for many apparently conflicting opinions as to when the country became an industrialized society. Pointing to the majority of people on farms in 1860, many scholars have said that it was still agricultural. The theme of this study has been the intensive industrialization of the northeastern seaboard, which by 1850 from the Merrimack River in New Hampshire to the Chesapeake Bay in Maryland had become a highly developed industrial area on a par with or ahead of similar regions in Britain or northwestern Europe. But unlike that of any nation in Europe development in the northeastern United States was based largely on rural waterpower, and the region was on the fringe of a vast, contiguous fertile area characterized by sparse population, continuous migration, and many areas of local economic development.

In Europe people preserved traditional tastes and ways of life. Many of them wanted handmade articles of a familiar style; maximum utility or productivity was often ignored. In America the mingling of immigrants and the movement of general population had made traditional tastes among the common people hard to preserve; settlers wanted what was most useful and durable for its price. Hence it may be said that Europe modified industrialism to fit its various cultures, while American culture more readily changed to suit new conditions. Europe seemed far away to the average American. Imports, other than books, tropical commodities, and special metals, were chiefly better-grade textiles and luxury goods. The basic utilities of life were made at home. Thus the "industrial society" in America differed in many ways from the advanced nations of Europe.

I

The relation of people to their work, for example, was different in a nation of continual in-migration, very rapid expansion, and population growth from that in countries of out-migration, with fixed boundaries and only gradual increase in numbers. And, of course, the relation to work in mills, factories, or large urban shops differed from that in Old World regions devoted primarily to agriculture and trade. Furthermore, the ability of youths to choose between local farming as a worker or tenant, migration to the developing West, or employment in industry made for high rates of turnover for the unskilled and general instability in particular job relationships among the skilled.

The supply of new labor for shops and mills also varied within the United States—among the different regions in the Northeast and among different periods of time. In New England, except for parts of Connecticut close to the port of New York, factory workers appear to have come in the early years chiefly from poor hill farms that forced members of expanding families to move either west or into industry. In Rhode Island, the most thoroughly industrialized state by 1810, immigrants were not an important source of workers before 1830. In Massachusetts and New Hampshire too, immigrants probably played a minor role during this period, as backcountry youth were deliberately recruited for mill work. Peter J. Coleman's statement that in Rhode Island the "cottage spinners and weavers, saw- and gristmillers, tanners, coopers, iron-workers, shoemakers, candlemakers, charcoal burners, and all manner of workers in wood had by 1800 come to constitute that reservoir of skill and experience essential to the launching of large scale industrial experimentation," was true of the Northeast Coast in general.[1] In addition to a supply of labor, all the large ports had the mercantile capital and men with the business experience necessary for the new ventures of this period.

In New York and Pennsylvania, the chief areas of American industrial employment, the labor situation before the 1830s differed from that in New England. In the Middle States rapidly developing industry had to compete with expanding agriculture. Growth along the Hudson, Mohawk, Passaic, Brandywine, Schuylkill, and Susquehanna rivers, as well as new iron and coal operations in the hinterland, held back the flow of "poor hill farmers" to the seaport industrial areas. Immigrants, arriving either through the ports of New York or Philadelphia or indirectly by way of Canada, appear to have been the major source of early labor for rapidly expanding mills.

Proof that the urban labor supply in the Middle States before 1820 was primarily immigrant has to be assembled from company payrolls and estimates by contemporaries. Federal immigration statistics start only on October 1, 1819, and then fail to record the subsequent movement of immigrants within the United States. The flow must have started as prosperity came to the Northeast Coast in the early 1790s. In 1794 a British traveler reported that in northern New Jersey near New York City, "Plenty ask for work."[2] Records for the Brandywine Valley near Wilmington, which Harold Hancock has called "the most important milling center in the United States" by 1800, show a work force drawn chiefly from Irish immigrants.[3] This continued to be the case up to and beyond 1820. Similarly, the nearby mill area on Chester Creek, midway between Wilmington and Philadelphia, also depended on immigrants.[4] When bad harvests in Europe temporarily stepped up immigration to the United States, as in 1801, "the streets of New York and Philadelphia swarmed with newcomers offering to employers all the labor they needed," as Marcus L. Hanson has put it; a surplus that lasted until, at least, 1803. Resumption of war in Europe made the newcomers more exclusively Irish and German, but the relatively heavy flow continued until 1812 and resumed in 1815, reaching an estimated 30,000 in 1818.[5]

Obviously Britain's efforts to prevent the emigration of mechanics were almost completely unsuccessful. There were no statistics available to authorities to prove a man's occupation, and Irishmen, Welshmen, Scotsmen, and Englishmen left Lancashire and other industrial areas to come to the United States. In truth, they probably hoped to become American farmers, as they stated on their British exit papers, but many or probably most of them knew they would have to work in mills or shops for a while in order to save the small amount of money necessary to travel from seaport to backcountry and perhaps begin farming as a tenant. The Brandywine and Chester Creek records show about a 50 percent a year turnover in labor, and often indicate a transition to farming.

The only federal statistics on immigrants before 1819 came by chance because of the War of 1812. About July 1, 1812, the State Department demanded that all male enemy aliens over fourteen years old register with the marshals in their state, giving age, length of residence, and occupation. In 1813 the department required that any of these men living within forty miles of tidewater had to file a petition in order to be allowed to stay. Of the original 1812 lists, those for Connecticut and New Hampshire were lost, and for Pennsylvania we have only about a third. In all, perhaps 10,000 originally registered, but the records of only 7,500 remain, and they are slanted against measuring industrial employment because of the losses in Connecticut, New Hampshire, and Pennsylvania. Nevertheless, about half of the existing records indicate industrial employment, with textile work in the lead.[6]

With the coming of annual records, federal statistics show a concentration of the immigrant flow to the entry ports of the Middle States. For the initial year 1819–20, New York City received 37 percent of the entries, Philadelphia 20 percent, Baltimore 13 percent, Boston 9 percent, and the rest were scattered. As the decade wore on more of the immigrants came through the port of New York, and the Middle States total rose to as high as 82 percent in 1824–25.[7] In 1839–40, a high year, the number of immigrants exceeded 92,000, with 72,000 arriving through the three big Middle States ports. The tendency of the Irish and Canadians to migrate to New England became strong only in the 1840s, when starving Irish rural workers were given government assistance to emigrate and, aside from ports in Canada, Boston was the nearest large American city and the cheapest to reach.

Since Stanley Lebergott finds that the foreign-born worked primarily in nonfarm jobs, it seems probable that most of the new shop, mill, and factory workers in the major coastal manufacturing areas of the Middle States either came from Europe or were second-generation urban Americans.[8] Consequently, the problem of what wage would attract native farm workers to industry was not important in this region. Rates of pay may have been set in some years by intercity competition, but in general wages for the unskilled seemed to conform to rather traditional levels that were probably just high enough to attract unemployed migrants to jobs.

Wage rates for labor concern us here chiefly in their possible effects on sectional growth, on consumer demand, and on who shared most from the rising standard of living generated by industrialization. Such effects are difficult to determine, however, for at least three reasons:

there are no reliable statistics on employment by specific occupation from 1790 to 1850; the wage rates for different occupations have to be derived from a few payroll records; and finally there is no way to estimate accurately all the changes in the cost of living.[9]

The problem of the number of workers by general occupation, always difficult to project from one census to another because of changing classifications, can only be stated in rather meaningless terms and fairly reliably only for 1820. This census categorized workers in agriculture, commerce, and industry. On this basis New York and Pennsylvania each had 60,000 industrial workers, Massachusetts 33,000, and Virginia 32,000. Rhode Island, with only 6,000, had the highest percentage of industrial workers in relation to its total population. In the 1820 figures the six leading states show an average of 4.5 percent of the population listed as employed in industry. But the census returns were quite inaccurate for industry, and a new census for that sector taken in 1822 had little more success, particularly in the Middle States.

To readers in the twentieth century the census category "employed in industry" may be misleading. Even in 1840 the majority in this category, particularly among urban workers, were in semiskilled or skilled crafts or laborers in small operations. While from 1794 on, the wage for laborers in Philadelphia was usually a dollar a day, truly skilled workers, or "artisans," received an average of $1.60.[10] Consequently it is difficult to say what industrialization did to the living standards of urban workers. Before 1840, at least, urban industry undoubtedly opened new opportunities and increased the number of semiskilled and skilled workers both in and out of plants, who except during periods of severe inflation appear to have received satisfactory compensation. From 1827 to 1837 the artisan labor movements chiefly emphasized free schools, more favorable laws for debtors, and the ten-hour day; then the inflation of the mid-1830s forced them to demand higher wages.

Whatever conclusions are reached concerning the effect of industrialization on those directly involved, the more important immediate social effect was on the much larger group employed in agriculture. Turnpikes and canals, for example, benefited both farm producers and urban consumers. Textile mills, by suppressing household spinning and weaving, had a mixed effect varying with whether or not the working time released could be used on the farm. Better farm machinery and equipment greatly helped those who used them; while these farmers appear to have been a rather small minority up to 1850, their numbers probably equaled the number of workers in highly mechanized industry.

Southerners casting a disapproving look northward, as well as contemporary observers in England looking at industrialization on their side of the Atlantic, argued that the lowest-paid workers were worse off with the coming of industrialization than they had been when confined to agriculture. One of the chief British attacks was on the filthy industrial city, begrimed with the smoke of factories dependent on steampower and soft coal. American cities, in contrast, were spared being buried in soot because most big users of power were located in the countryside and by the 1830s anthracite coal was the fuel for heating. Labor journalists in the United States, particularly in the 1830s, focused on wages. They argued that while wages for skilled labor rose somewhat with prices, machines were reducing the need for such men, and, therefore, they, too had been better off in the societies depending chiefly on handicrafts, agriculture, and commerce. Yet the direct substitution of unskilled for skilled labor appears to have been uncommon in practice; rather the total nonfarm labor force grew rapidly.[11]

II

It is apparent from available figures that some employers of unskilled labor were able to establish wages that varied little or not at all with changes in the cost of living. Fixed wages seem to have been the case among such diverse workers as textile mill hands, urban porters, and shipyard laborers. From 1794 to 1830 ship repair records put unskilled wages at one dollar a day, very high in comparison to other wage series, and in only six years was there a temporary downward deviation from this high norm. On the other hand, a table of "real" daily wages for laborers adjusted to a cost of living index, also by Donald R. Adams, Jr., but drawn from other data, shows variations, gradually upward, from 50 cents a day in 1790 to $1.05 in 1829. According to this same cost of living index, the secular trend of prices was sharply upward from 1793 to 1814 and downward from then to 1830, with the biggest drop from 1818 to 1819.[12] From 1830 to 1839 prices again rose; then they fell sharply to 1844. Wage analysts in general find Philadelphia area rates usually, but not always, higher than those in eastern Massachusetts. They also find immigrants more likely to seek the higher wage areas than the native-born.

Any discussion of employment in factories using power machinery inevitably emphasizes cotton textiles, a highly labor-intensive industry and one from which many mill records remain. While some ironworks had over five hundred employees, their records are fragmentary. Wages in textile mills have been subject to more study than wages in other industries, and conclusions from them as to unskilled rates seem fairly reliable. From 1815 to 1840 the so-called boarding house system used in the large mills in Massachusetts and southern New Hampshire, controlled by a group of socially prominent Boston merchants, attracted much attention. Girls willing to leave home signed contracts with traveling mill agents, usually to work for at least a year at $2.50 per week, less $1.25 for board.[13] The boarding houses were well run, and the girls could apparently save money for dowries or other future needs. But with inflation in the 1830s, and no increase in pay, these jobs became less desirable; ultimately Canadian and Irish immigrants replaced native farm girls.

A short trip from Boston, where so many visitors entered the United States via the Cunard Line, the Lowell mills were something of a tourist attraction and came to typify American industrialism for Europeans and Americans alike. But in reality they and the other large boarding house mills in half a dozen Massachusetts or New Hampshire cities differed greatly from the usual American mill or factory. The average textile mill in 1840 was small, employed perhaps sixty or so workers, and was probably supervised by a proprietor.[14] In contrast, supervision, by hired managers, was stricter in the Lowell-type mills because of their young female employees. While most waterpowered textile mills, such as those at Rockdale, Pennsylvania, were located in the countryside, large cities grew around the clusters of Boston-owned mills in Massachusetts and New Hampshire. Yet these cities, where only a small amount of coal was burned, usually anthracite and limited to heating purposes, were relatively clean compared to the centers of the British steampowered textile industry, such as Manchester and Leeds, and British visitors were always greatly impressed. The visitors also had official escorts who passed over the strict controls exercised on the life of the workers as benevolent paternalism. Area-wide blacklists for troublemakers and unduly long hours at some times of the year were, of course, never mentioned.

Along the rest of the Northeast Coast the so-called family system was the rule in textile mills. A man with some skill could command a wage of $4 to $6 dollars a week, a woman $2 dollars, and children from 50 cents to a dollar. Thus a couple with two working children could bring in over $8 a week.[15] These rates seemed to apply to Delaware and Pennsylvania as well as to Connecticut and Rhode Island, and to 1810 as well as to 1830 or 1840.[16]

Complete mills had mule spinners, weavers, and various other specialists or foremen who earned $8 to $10 a week.[17] But by 1840 automatic looms, self-acting mules, and other improvements in textile machinery were reducing the percentage of skilled labor in mills. Scholars estimate that in the 1820s unskilled wages in America were about one-fifth higher than in Britain, but skilled wages were about the same.[18] From these facts some economists have deduced a special American pressure to displace unskilled labor with machines, but case studies suggest that the trend toward mechanization came more from cultural and managerial bias than from carefully calculated marginal costs.

Whether the skilled mill or factory worker was better off than the journeyman artisan is impossible to estimate. In many cases the transition from small shop to large factory was a gradual one, involving an increasing division of labor and the introduction of new machines. While the major industries of building and ship construction introduced such innovations as the balloon frame house and the steamer, many of the categories of work involved in manufacturing new products remained essentially the same. As agricultural and industrial productivity rose, food and household wares became cheaper in relation to wages, but this shift was not rapid before 1840.

Both Stanley Lebergott and Jeffrey G. Williamson have estimated real income and its distribution. Lebergott finds a 17 percent increase in real wages for the unskilled between 1820 and 1850, or about one-half of a percent a year. The work of both scholars indicates that the employed unskilled did relatively well in poor times and less well in boom periods. Dividing urban population between the "poor," or the unskilled, and all others, Williamson estimates that from 1820 to 1856 the real wages of the poor increased 82 percent, but the income of the upper urban groups increased substantially more.[19]

An intermediate group of semiskilled workers continued to ply their crafts in the cities long after machines were also being used for similar work. Three thousand handloom weavers worked in two sections of Philadelphia in 1850. Many had learned weaving while in prison for vagrancy or small crimes. Shoemaking was also a craft that required few tools and could easily be mastered. The list might be expanded to such crafts as baking, blacksmithing, construction, gardening, printing, or tinworking, with some men claiming mastery of two or more of these "skills."[20]

No matter what the industry, the change in life styles involved in moving from farm to factory was not easy. In evaluating the many arguments on the effect of early industrialization on the unskilled worker, however, one must also remember the alternatives. Life on the farm was hard, too. The twelve-hour day, maintained in part to keep workers under control, did not appear as a major deterrent to recruitment of farm labor in New England or a discourager of immigration to the Middle States. In general, mill work was less demanding of strength and close attention than farm work. On farms, as soon as children had sufficient strength, they were assigned chores that kept them busy most of their waking hours. Consequently the twelve-hour day of children in shop or mill did not seem as horrendous then as it does now. There were also compensations in more varied companionship, participation in social activities, and personal independence in leisure hours. Twelve-year olds who worked in mills when they might have been in school may have preferred the mill with its atmosphere of sharing tasks with adults. By the 1830s new machinery was displacing child labor in the textile industry, where most children were employed.

More attention has been given to the conditions of the most low paid than to those of the skilled, because the condition of the former was subject to the criticism of southern planters seeking to defend slavery and of social reformers in both America and Europe. Certainly, by comparison to conditions in the later, high-wage period of industrialization, conditions in the early period left much room for improvement. The majority of unskilled shop or mill workers lived an insecure existence. Yet the evidence indicates that they had plenty of food, including meat and fish, and possibly too much untaxed liquor. To middle-class reformers factory workers might seem oppressed by dictatorial overseers, low pay, and paternalistic controls, but the continuing supply of such labor suggests that to Irish or German immigrants, or to girls and boys bored with the closed existence of the farm, the jobs were attractive. In addition, expanding industry and trade continually increased the types of available jobs. It should also be remembered that at this stage of industrialization skilled workers or artisans in city shops or factories who received more than subsistence wages probably outnumbered the unskilled. Furthermore, lack of skill was associated with youth, and many workers acquired skills and increased their pay as they grew older.

The strong movement for the ten-hour day arose only in the 1820s, and then it was led by artisans, not mill workers. The workday was regularly broken by a half hour for breakfast and usually three-quarters of an hour for dinner. There were also shorter breaks for coffee, cakes, or candy.[21] Although for those needing eight hours sleep there was little time left for reading, poor education and flickering candlelight in preindustrial years had never encouraged the habit. The classic question of whether or not industrialization benefited the worker, therefore, is not amenable to a single, comprehensive answer.

Urban lighting was improved by gas made from bituminous coal from the 1820s on, but the only good source of light on the farm remained whale oil, too expensive for poorer families. The kerosene lamp that made lighting cheap and practically universal came only after 1860. Early in the century the increased scale of metalwork brought specialized household utensils such as grinders and presses within the reach of the working-class family. As Dorothy S. Brady has pointed out, "Pillows and mattresses, by-products of the textile industry, were a significant part of the more comfortable image that drew immigrants across the Atlantic." By 1830 a housewife could buy the material for a full-length mattress for $1.70.[22] In the 1830s the balloon frame house, made of wooden siding supported by two-by-four studs and beams, took the place of log, brick, or stone construction in many areas and put structures of more than two rooms within reach of farm and industrial families.

In spite of iron stoves, conditions of heat and cold seem to have been as intolerable in the mills as in farmhouses. Since for spinning and weaving moderate temperatures were desirable, there was some heating in these mills. All types of mills were dusty, drafty, and noisy, and the air in textile mills was full of lint. Few mills had exhaust fans, and no one knows how much of the widespread tuberculosis was caused by polluted air. In this instance high labor turnover, running around 50 percent a year and often or perhaps usually indicating a return to agriculture, may have been a saving element in preserving health. On Chester Creek, Pennsylvania, only 10 percent of workers stayed at one job for a decade.[23]

Since mills using waterpower, whether for production of iron, paper, gunpowder, woodworking, or textiles, were in country locations, housing and food had to be supplied by the proprietors. Hence paternalism was inevitable in the waterpowered mill. Furthermore, lack of any public transportation combined with long hours of work and short breaks for lunch and dinner meant that housing had to be within a few minutes walk of the mill. Low rents of a dollar or two a month were a part of the paternalistic package, for higher rents would have had to be reflected in wage rates. In order to provide cheap housing for the un-married, the three-story stone or brick quarters typical in the Middle States, with a room on each floor, were often rented only to families who would agree to take in at least two boarders. Since the cost of food for a man in the Delaware Valley area about 1830 has been estimated at 15 cents a day, a family taking boarders at $2 a week for a man or $1.50 for a woman could show a good profit.[24]

If mill work was to be an avenue to farming further west, a family had to be able to save money. For a family of four workers, and perhaps a boarder, this was clearly possible in the mills whose records have been studied. Anthony F. C. Wallace says that it was possible for working people, particularly in the mills, "to live well and save money." Some of his evidence shows the transition to farming was easier than suggested by the opponents of the old theory that the frontier was a "safety valve" for the unemployed. In 1836, a boom year in real estate, a family of four moved from a Chester Creek mill to Ohio. They bought a 120-acre farm, a pig, and two sows, and hired help to build a log cabin, all for $200 they had saved from the family wages.[25]

While saving was possible, perhaps easy for the right-sized family when work was continuous and food prices were low, there were frequent shutdowns by the mills and rigid wages even when prices rose sharply. Poor family management or intemperance or some mixture of both probably kept the average mill family from accumulating long-term credit on the books.[26] But a lack of savings did not mean that im-poverished workers could not move into agriculture, for single males often went as hired hands and families as tenants. There were frequent shifts between farm and mill that depended on seasonal opportunities and the relative prosperity of each sector.[27]

The mill operator also had to supply general stores where food, liquor, and dry goods could be bought on credit pending the monthly payday. For workers wanting to drink with companions there were small unlicensed taverns in the woods, also selling on credit and permitted to exist by millers and the local authorities. If the workers accumulated savings, they could be deposited at either the store or the paymaster's office; an interest of 6 percent was earned on the balance. It was from such accounts that frugal families bought farms, sometimes on land owned by the mill proprietors where easy terms of payment were offered. Mills also had to have doctors nearby, who might be paid by owners for treating accidents, or by the patients for ordinary illnesses. Similarly, company aid was often available to workers involved with the law.[28]

Lengthy discussion of country mills should not obscure the fact that as industrialization grew, more and more of the workers were in cities, where there were greater freedom, less paternalism, and more workers earning relatively high wages. While in 1820 New York and Boston were still chiefly interested in trade and shipping, Baltimore and Philadelphia were industrial cities. The extremely rapid growth of all these cities from 1820 to 1850 produced new and increasing social problems. They needed sewage, better water, police and fire protection, public health authorities, and education, but, except for Boston late in the period, the cities did little to meet these needs. The municipal governments were risk-taking organizations hoping by good luck to avoid such disasters as epidemics, devastating fires, or riots. It is not the purpose of this study to discuss social problems, but much of the dismal picture of early industrialization held by its opponents in America and abroad comes from the untended and unplanned big city.[29]

III

With no secret ballot, employees in both city and countryside found it wise to support the ticket of their employers. Although conscientious operators such as E. I. du Pont always protested that the workers were not subject to any employer pressures, solid votes against candidates regarded as inimical to the interests of the company suggest otherwise.[30] Similar coercion was practiced in other industrial areas.[31] Since busy factory or mill owners were likely to be apolitical on many issues, the pressure on workers was intermittent rather than continuous.

Industrialization did not greatly alter politics in the seaport cities except for, after 1815, the acceptance of an occasional manufacturer among the mercantile and financial elites that had always been in control. The gradual movement from direct participation by these elites on urban councils to their representation by professional politicians, which occurred rapidly in the 1820s, was a product of increasing urban size and increasing demand for urban services such as water, street paving, police, and gas that made city affairs too time-consuming for control by businessmen. Although urbanization and industrialization went hand in hand, cities would have developed in much the same direction on account of population increases and improvements in transportation even in the old handicraft system.

The same generalizations apply to state politics. The large investments in finance and transportation by New York and Pennsylvania were a response to farmers wanting access to markets and an expanding commercial system rather than to factory industry. Albany and Troy, for example, became manufacturing centers partly because of the Mohawk Canal of 1796, but the canal was financed to bring upstate farm products to the port of New York, not to benefit manufactures. The frenzy of the mid-1820s over connections to the West, which led to two Massachusetts railroads, the Pennsylvania Mainline system, and the Maryland canal and railroad, was inspired more by merchants who feared loss of trade if they did not keep up with rival ports than by manufacturers foreseeing a great western market for factory products—one that, in fact, was not important before the 1840s. The backcountry farm counties in all the northeastern states, save Delaware and New Jersey, continued until mid-century successfully to oppose most laws and taxes designed specifically to aid the large urban areas.

All of these crosscurrents did not add up to governments unfavorable to business; they were, in fact, quite the opposite, but it was from friendliness to backcountry enterprises as well as to urban commerce rather than from any special affinity for manufacturing. Although Massachusetts led the way in encouraging the incorporation of manufacturing companies by the general act of 1809, which granted a uniform charter to all legal applicants, only a few large industrial enterprises, in any of the states, actually applied for incorporation. Instead, northeastern industries in general, and the coal and iron industries of the Middle States in particular, benefited indirectly from State and local aid to canals and railroads.

As already seen, the state courts gave increasing support to the law of contract, with the most dramatic assertion of the inviolability of corporate charters coming in the *Dartmouth College* decision of the United States Supreme Court in 1820. Four years later, in *Gibbons v. Ogden*, the high court held federal power over interstate commerce to be inviolable by the states. In *Bank of Augusta v. Earle* (1839) the Supreme

Court affirmed the right of corporations to do business in any state unless forbidden by a specific law. But all of these decisions might, and probably would, have been reached had there been no development of mechanized industry. The same could be said regarding the poorly operated patent policy up to 1836.[32] The one federal policy that from 1816 on depended on expanding industrialization was, as described in chapter 5, the protective tariff. And even here the effects of the legislation on desirable industrial growth and vice versa were, and have continued to be, a matter of controversy.

The real impact of industrial business on political decisions grew with the railroad age, particularly from the early 1840s on. In contrast to the largest manufacturers, even small railroads kept full-time lobbyists at the state capitals and joined in supporting both lobbyists and politicians in Washington. It was the steady pressures from railroad interests, year after year, that paved the way for the defensive political strength of industrial business in the latter half of the nineteenth century.

IV

Up to 1840 the effect of industrialization on education was small. The need for educated clerks was supplied by middle-class youths who attended the traditional types of private academies or evening business schools in the major cities. Employers generally failed to recognize the value of education for manual workers, beyond apprenticeship or on-the-job training. While this was probably an error in collective business judgment, the state of technology at the time made it hard to make a case for geography, higher mathematics, or the sciences. The level of elementary education in 1800 was probably below that of 1775.[33]

In spite of lip service to education in political speeches, Newton Edwards and Herman G. Richey have noted that "there was little evidence that schools were generally considered as necessary means of solving political, economic and social problems of the day." Outside of New England, early state constitutions had few provisions regarding education. James G. Carter, a writer on education, thought in 1824 that American education had declined during the early nineteenth century.[34]

In the 1830s elementary school systems in Prussia, France, and Scotland were held up as models by reformers in an effort to stimulate state action, but the major force behind public education laws from the 1820s on was urban growth. Middle-class city dwellers feared a populace not indoctrinated with respect for law and order. Since cities were a part of the industrial complex, industrialization might be seen as indirectly bringing action. The action, however, was limited. Various state laws establishing public education had either local option clauses, as in Pennsylvania, or provisions for town payments to the state in lieu of maintaining a school, as in Massachusetts. Yet interest in the whole problem of education was growing and was unquestionably higher in New England than in the Middle States or the West. But the proponents of public schools placed more emphasis on their indoctrinating good citizenship than on economic benefits.[35]

After the turn of the century millowners made some efforts at supporting evening or Sunday schools, but one must remember that the great majority of children were brought up on farms where education followed hereditary patterns: well-educated parents teaching their children, even in the absence of schools, and poorly educated parents not encouraging the education of their children, even in the presence of schools. Itinerant teachers visited farm neighborhoods only every few years. Many Americans who could sign their names and decipher simple sentences lacked the ability to read at a level that would make it enjoyable or productive. Farmers could not see the value of higher taxes to support public schools. New York and Philadelphia had pauper schools, but their obvious social stigma limited attendance.

That free elementary schooling advanced more rapidly just before and after mid-century is partly due to the business boom from 1843 to 1854, but also to the persuasive abilities of the Boston lawyer, Horace Mann. Mann left his law practice to help create a Massachusetts board of education in 1837 and as its secretary to persuade businessmen that "education has a market value; that it is so far an article of merchandise, that it may be turned to a pecuniary account; it may be minted and will yield a larger amount of statutable coin than common bullion."[36] In report after report, including the widely read Fifth Report (1842), Mann kept emphasizing the value to business of free education. And gradually he persuaded businessmen, starting with those in Massachusetts, of the truth of his argument. By 1850 the northeastern United States had joined the world's leaders in free elementary education.

Outside of Massachusetts there were no requirements for public high schools, and even there such schools amounted to only one or two teacher institutions. The middle class, those directing the course of industrialization and receiving its profits, could afford to send their children to academies or business schools, and they preferred to pay tuition for a few years rather than school taxes for a lifetime. Both texts and curriculums in the private academies, however, moved gradually in the direction of meeting the requirements of business. Books on mathematics cited examples from bookkeeping, and courses on statistics, technology, drawing, engineering, mapmaking, and geography were offered in the few schools where there was someone competent to teach one or more such subjects. But, by and large, full-time secondary education remained a preparation for classical college curriculums.

Clerks and other beginners in commerce could also attend private night schools, soon to be called business colleges, for short courses. Such institutions went back to the early eighteenth century, but the establishment of James A. Bennett's bookkeeping school in New York City in 1818 marks the beginning of a great expansion. Two years later Bennett published *Bookkeeping Adapted to the Commerce of the United States and Exemplified in One Set of Books*, which went through fifteen editions within a decade. By the 1840s three-month evening courses were available at a score of business colleges in the major cities.[37]

Thus the frontiers of change in education that developed from the expanding economic system were, before 1850, chiefly on the level of secondary education and much more for the benefit of potential businessmen than of manual workers either skilled or unskilled. This bias was probably inherent in the business-industrial pattern. Office skills and useful administrative information could be taught, whereas technological dexterity could usually be acquired most reliably from experience.

The effect of the advancing economy on higher education was also slight. West Point and Rensselaer Polytechnic Institute remained the only engineering schools. Led by Harvard in the late 1820s, major universities started law schools, introduced economics under the guise of moral philosophy, and taught some physical science, but otherwise their cleric-dominated boards of trustees saw little association between college education and the economic frontiers of change. While improved management may have accounted for a large part of the increased productivity from 1790 to 1850, the effectiveness of this segment of "human capital" must have been increased more from experience than from formal education.

V

"The basic value system, as solidified in the early days of the nation," writes Seymour Lipset, "can account for the kind of changes that have taken place in American character and American institutions, as these faced the need to adjust to the requirements of an urban, industrial, bureaucratic society."[38] In the industrial Northeast of 1850, adjustment to the first two requirements was well advanced; in fact Perry Miller believes the regional culture was dominated by the values of expanding business as early as 1815, but Lipset's third change—adjustment to bureaucratic forms in management and politics—was only beginning.[39] Among the issues of mid-century, the journalist Henry V. Poor was correct in identifying managerial adjustment to the demands of railroads, and necessarily to other large multiunit business structures, as an unsolved problem and one calling for abilities different from those required in the American past.

The technological revolution had occurred and had been welcomed. Previous chapters have illustrated the avidity with which American mechanics seized on new and useful technology, reproduced it to their own liking, and put it to work more quickly, relative to their knowledge and opportunities, than their counterparts elsewhere in the world. The industrialization that occurred in and around the major cities of the Middle States before 1810 could have been, if necessary, largely independent from that going on in Britain at the same time.

The quick adaptation of machinery from abroad and the improvization of new machines at home were based on cultural values gained from the American experience in migrating and settling part of a continent. Cities and towns built by migrants had an unusually high percentage of young men. These men were adventurous or they would not have migrated, and the very fact of living in a new setting was strongly conducive to innovation.[40]

The people who remained in the older nations brought no such background to the critical period of physical innovation that began in the eighteenth century. The unprecedented speed of the utilization of resources for industrial purposes in America, therefore, was the result of a favorable cultural heritage brought to bear on new physical problems. Each nation, to be sure, had its strengths and weaknesses. The French invented many new principles and processes, but characteristics of their culture and environment made them slow in practical adaptations. Britain led the world in the division of labor in metalwork as early as 1750, only to have the heritage of such high and circumscribed skills become a hinderance to more complete mechanization. The United States had resources in wood and waterpower generally lacking in Europe, and particularly in Britain. It also had a desire for the new, and workers with moderate skills at a great many tasks that made for a flexible labor force ready to pursue novel enterprises.[41] The result was the highly pragmatic, make-do-and-get-the-goods-out character of American production. In all, the progress of industrialization throughout the world was determined less by national leaders and followers than by distinct specialties arising from the culture, geography, and resources of each nation.

Notes

Introduction

1. Paul A. David says, "It is necessary to discard neoclassical traditions in favor of an explicitly historical vision." *Technical Choice, Innovation and Economic Growth*, p. 10.
2. Jacob Schmookler, *Invention and Economic Growth*, p. 12.

1. Why America and Britain?

1. Joel Mokyr, "Demand vs. Supply in the Industrial Revolution," p. 989.
2. J. R. Harris, *Industry and Technology in the Eighteenth Century*.
3. For Wallace's definition, see his *Culture and Personality*, p. 112; for Goodenough, Tylor, and others, see Milton Singer, "Culture," 3:538. For more discussion, see Louis Schneider and Charles M. Bonjean, eds., *The Idea of Culture in the Social Sciences*. For a similar approach in the terminology of sociology, see Neil Smelser, *Social Change in the Industrial Revolution*, chaps. 1–3.
4. John U. Nef, *Cultural Foundations of Industrial Civilization*.
5. Sanichiro Mizushima rests his argument chiefly on cultural preparation. "Background of Modernization in Japan," pp. 166–67.
6. William Barrett, *Time of Need*, p. 73.
7. Morton J. Horwitz, *The Transformation of American Law, 1780–1860*.
8. Billy G. Smith, "Death and Life in a Colonial Immigrant City," pp. 373–75.
9. Stanley Bailis, "The Development and Significance of Role-Modification Directives under Rapid Socio-Cultural Change," pp. 75, 85, 115–18.
10. Robert G. Albion, *The Rise of New York Port, 1815–1860*, pp. 285–86.

2. A Business Basis for Industrialism

1. Gary Lawson Brown, *Baltimore in the Nation, 1789–1861*, p. 85.
2. Carville V. Earle and Ronald A. Hoffman, "Commerce and Labor."
3. Ronald L. Lewis, *Coal, Iron and Slaves*.
4. Joseph Stancliffe Davis, *Essays in the Earlier History of American Corporations*, 1:4.
5. George Heberton Evans, Jr., *Business Incorporations in the United States, 1800–1943*, p. 14.
6. Diane Lindstrom, *Economic Development in the Philadelphia Region, 1810–1850*.
7. Most of the generalizations regarding the relations between state and federal doctrines come from Tony A. Freyer, *Forums of Order*.
8. Horwitz, *Transformation of American Law*, pp. 2.
9. Ibid., pp. 11, 23, 3, 24.
10. Oscar Handlin and Mary Flug Handlin, *Commonwealth*, pp. 145–46.
11. Freyer, *Forums of Order*, p. 28.
12. Horwitz, *Transformation of American Law*, p. 20.
13. Freyer, *Forums of Order*, p. 67.
14. Harold D. Woodman, *King Cotton and His Retainers*, pp. 10ff.
15. Freyer, *Forums of Order*, pp. 53–98.
16. Horwitz, *Transformation of American Law*, p. 224.
17. Charles Warren, *Bankruptcy in United States History*, pp. 6ff.
18. Louis Hartz, *Economic Policy and Democratic Thought*, p. 237.
19. Peter J. Coleman, *Debtors and Creditors in America*, p. 256; quotation from p. 287.
20. Warren, *Bankruptcy in United States History*, pp. 19–20.
21. Coleman, *Debtors and Creditors*, pp. 32–34.
22. Ibid., pp. 104, 34–37.
23. Ibid., p. 288.
24. Warren, *Bankruptcy in United States History*, pp. 56ff.; see also Hartz, *Economic Policy and Democratic Thought*, pp. 227–29.
25. Warren, *Bankruptcy in United States History*, p. 81.
26. Coleman, *Debtors and Creditors*, p. 23.
27. Warren, *Bankruptcy in United States History*, pp. 87–88; Hartz, *Economic Policy and Democratic Thought*, pp. 229–35.
28. Coleman, *Debtors and Creditors*, p. 285.
29. Quoted in N. S. B. Gras, *The Massachusetts First National Bank of Boston, 1784–1934*, p. 43.
30. Bray Hammond, *Banks and Politics in America from the Revolution to the Civil War*, pp. 76–77.
31. Henry W. Domett, *A History of the Bank of New York, 1784–1884*, p. 12.
32. Hartz, *Economic Policy and Democratic Thought*, p. 83.
33. J. Van Fenstermaker, *The Development of American Commercial Banking, 1782–1837*, p. 16.
34. Paul R. Trescott, *Financing American Enterprise*, p. 19.

35. Richard Sylla, "American Banking and Growth in the Nineteenth Century," p. 219.
36. Herman Krooss, "Financial Institutions," p. 106.
37. For more detail, see Donald R. Adams, Jr., *Finance and Enterprise in Early America.*
38. Quoted in Margaret G. Myers, *The New York Money Market,* 1:6.
39. Fritz Redlich, *The Molding of American Banking,* 1:213.
40. Roy F. Foulke, *Sinews of American Commerce,* p. 129.
41. Roy J. Sampson, "American Accounting Education Textbooks and Public Practice prior to 1900," p. 461.
42. Stuart Bruchey, *Robert Oliver, Merchant of Baltimore,* pp. 135–39.
43. Myers, *New York Money Market,* 1:17.
44. Albert O. Greef, *The Commercial Paper House in the United States,* pp. 7–16.

3. The Patterns of Trade

1. Paul A. David, "New Light on a Statistical Dark Age," p. 48.
2. Peter Mathias, "Capital, Credit and Enterprise in the Industrial Revolution," p. 126.
3. Handlin and Handlin, *Commonwealth,* p. 60.
4. Brown, *Baltimore in the Nation,* pp. 26–30.
5. Allan R. Pred, *Urban Growth and the Circulation of Information,* p. 124.
6. Timothy Pitkin, *A Statistical View of the Commerce of the United States of America,* pp. 35, 111.
7. David M. Ellis et al., *A Short History of New York State,* p. 174.
8. Gordon C. Bjork, "Foreign Trade," p. 57.
9. Stanley L. Engerman, "Douglas C. North's *The Economic Growth of the United States, 1790–1860* Revisited," pp. 250, 253.
10. Diane Lindstrom calls this emphasis "the Eastern demand model."
11. Elting E. Morison, *From Know-How to No-where,* pp. 23–30.
12. Peter Lane, *The Industrial Revolution,* pp. 162–66.
13. Caroline F. Ware, *The Early New England Cotton Manufacture,* p. 16; Ellis, *Short History of New York State,* p. 180.
14. Lane, *Industrial Revolution,* p. 162.
15. Ellis, *Short History of New York State,* p. 180.
16. Hartz, *Economic Policy and Democratic Thought,* pp. 100–103.
17. Sidney I. Pomerantz, *New York, An American City,* p. 162.
18. George R. Taylor, *The Transportation Revolution, 1815–1860* p. 70; see also Louis C. Hunter, *Steamboats on the Western Rivers.*
19. Pomerantz, *New York,* pp. 163–64; Pred, *Urban Growth,* pp. 178–80, 37.
20. Pred, *Urban Growth,* pp. 23ff.

4. New Methods of Production, 1785–1825

1. For the European background, see W. W. Rostow, *How It All Began,* pp. 22ff.

2. Nathan Rosenberg, *Perspectives on Technology*.
3. Robert Brooke Zevin, *The Growth of Manufacturing in Early Nineteenth-Century New England*, introduction.
4. David John Jeremy, "British Textile Technology Transition to the United States," pp. 36–37.
5. Robert P. Multhauf, "America's Wooden Age," p. 23; see also Brooke Hindle, ed., *America's Wooden Age*.
6. Donald R. Adams, Jr., "Some Evidence on English and American Wage Rates," p. 510. See also Nathan Rosenberg, "Anglo-American Wage Differentials in the 1820s," pp. 221–29. The two labor markets differed so much in quality that they are hard to compare.
7. H. J. Habakkuk, *American and British Technology in the Nineteenth Century*, p. 60.
8. Peter Mathias, *The First Industrial Nation*, p. 18.
9. Pred, *Urban Growth*, pp. 192–94.
10. Habakkuk, *American and British Technology*, p. 185.
11. Jacob E. Cooke, *Tench Coxe and the Early Republic*, p. 186.
12. Charles V. Hagnar, *Early History of the Falls of the Schuylkill, Manayunk, Schuylkill and Lehigh Navigation Companies*, p. 33.
13. Rosenberg, *Perspectives on Technology*, p. 51. Eugene S. Ferguson points out that in 1800 much American metalworking machinery was crude judged by British standards. "Technology as Knowledge," p. 13.
14. Quoted in Victor S. Clark, *History of Manufactures in the United States, 1607–1860*, 1:211.
15. Miriam Hussey, *From Merchants to "Colour Men,"* pp. 2–4.
16. Daniel T. Rodgers, *The Work Ethic in Industrial America, 1850–1920*, p. 6.
17. Merritt Roe Smith, *Harpers Ferry Armory and the New Technology*.
18. Mathias, *First Industrial Nation*, pp. 129ff.
19. Rolla Milton Tryon, *Household Manufactures in the United States, 1640–1860*, pp. 162ff.
20. Ibid., p. 132.
21. Clark, *History of Manufactures*, 1:225–26.
22. Ware, *Early New England Cotton Manufacture*, p. 51.
23. Carl W. Condit, *American Building*, p. 44.
24. James Mease, M.D., *The Picture of Philadelphia*, p. 74.
25. Peter C. Welsh, "Tanning," pp. 10–16, 59.
26. Louis C. Hunter, *A History of Industrial Power in the United States, 1780–1930*, 1:455–69.
27. George Escol Sellers, *Early Engineering Reminiscences (1815–40) of George Escol Sellers*, p. 90.
28. Harold B. Hancock, "Delaware Papermakers and Papermaking, 1787–1840," p. 10; quotation from p. 9.
29. David C. Smith, *History of Papermaking in the United States (1691–1969)*, p. 30.
30. John W. Oliver, *History of American Technology*, p. 207.
31. John Leander Bishop, *A History of American Manufactures from 1608 to*

1860, 1:68. Calico printing was also being carried on in several places in Philadelphia by 1802. *New American State Papers*, 1:90–91.

32. John Palmer Garber, *The Valley of the Delaware and Its Place in American History*, p. 191.

33. *New American State Papers*, 1:39.

34. David B. Tyler, *The American Clyde*.

35. Marion V. Brewington, "Maritime Philadelphia, 1609–1837," p. 109; Augustus C. Buell, *The Memoirs of Charles H. Cramp*, pp. 23–31.

36. George S. Gibb, *The Saco-Lowell Shops*, pp. 46–76; Jeremy, "British Textile Technology Transition," pp. 41–43.

37. Robert D. Arbuckle, "John Nicholson and the Attempt to Promote Pennsylvania Manufacturing," pp. 99–116; Peter J. Coleman, *The Transformation of Rhode Island, 1790–1860*, pp. 77–78; David John Jeremy, "The Transmission of Cotton and Woollen Manufacturing Technologies between Britain and the United States of America from 1790 to the 1830s."

38. The warp is the thread through which the weft or woof is woven and needs more strength.

39. Ware, *Early New England Cotton Manufacture*, pp. 15–16, 158.

40. Ibid., p. 15.

41. Hunter reports the steampowered mill in *History of Industrial Power*, 1:435. Peter Temin calculates that as late as 1840 the direct costs of steampower were higher than for waterpower. "Steam and Waterpower in the Early Nineteenth Century," p. 204.

42. Clark, *History of Manufactures*, 1:453.

43. Carlton O. Wittlinger, "Early Manufacturing in Lancaster County, 1710–1840," pp. 115–16. See also John W. Lozier, "The Forgotten Industry."

44. Coleman, *Transformation of Rhode Island*, pp. 82ff.

45. Clark, *History of Manufactures*, 1:403.

46. Habakkuk, *American and British Technology*, p. 181.

47. Pred, *Urban Growth*, p. 258.

48. Will Holmes, "Early American Sawmills."

49. Habakkuk, *American and British Technology*, p. 121.

50. Eugene S. Ferguson, *The Americanness of American Technology*, p. 2.

51. Joseph Wickham Roe, *English and American Tool Builders*, p. 246.

52. Eugene S. Ferguson, *Oliver Evans*, and Greville Bathe and Dorothy Bathe, *Oliver Evans*.

53. Evans's book was called *The Abortion of the Young Steam Engineer's Guide*. The odd title resulted from the cantankerous Evans's quarrel with his publisher and was altered in a later edition. Ferguson, "Technology as Knowledge," p. 16. Ferguson's small volume on Evans has the most comprehensive view. See also Carroll W. Pursell, Jr., *Early Stationary Steam Engines in America*, and the biography of Evans by the Bathes.

54. John Fitch, *Autobiography of John Fitch*.

55. Dorothy Gregg, "John Stevens, General Entrepreneur."

56. Louis C. Hunter, "The Heroic Theory of Invention, pp. 25–39.

57. Encyclopedias that described older steam engines were available, plus a few

technical papers, but they only conveyed general principles. There is no indication that Fitch, Evans, or French depended on European master workmen. For number of boats in 1811, see Bishop, *History of American Manufactures*, 2:173–74.

58. Arthur Cecil Bining, *Pennsylvania Iron Manufacture in the Eighteenth Century*; B. F. French, *History of the Rise and Progress of the Iron Trade of the United States from 1621 to 1857*.

59. Robert B. Thomas, "A Study of the Industry in the Falls of the Schuylkill-Manayunk Area from the Colonial Era to the Civil War," pp. 13–23; Bishop, *History of American Manufactures*, 2:326.

60. Sellers, *Early Engineering Reminiscences*, pp. 112ff.

61. Quoted in Ferguson, "Technology as Knowledge," p. 21.

62. Sellers, *Early Engineering Reminiscences*, p. 26.

63. Paul Uselding, "Studies of Technology in Economic History," pp. 172–74.

64. Rosenberg, *Perspectives on Technology*, p. 99; Eugene S. Ferguson, introduction to Sellers, *Early Engineering Reminiscences*, p. iii.

65. Ferguson thinks this "open-shop" policy of exchange of information "close to the top of the list" of factors that advanced American mechanical knowhow. "Technology as Knowledge," p. 24. See also George S. Gibb, "The Pre-Industrial Revolution in America," p. 112.

66. Clark, *History of Manufactures*, 1:519.

67. Smith, *Harpers Ferry Armory*, pp. 34–67, 256.

68. Ibid., pp. 222–28.

69. Felicia Johnson Deyrup, *Arms Makers of the Connecticut Valley*, p. 37.

70. Hindle, *America's Wooden Age*.

71. Meyer H. Fishbein, "The Census of Manufactures, 1810–90," pp. 7–9. For a modern guess, see Barry W. Poulson, "Estimates of the Value of Manufacturing Output in the Early Nineteenth Century," pp. 522–23.

72. *New American State Papers*, 1:190–236. Poulson, using regression analysis, applied Robert E. Gallman's figures for 1840 as well as the census figures, and reckons a maximum error of 25 percent and a rank order similar to that stated in the text. "Estimates of the Value of Manufacturing."

73. Arbuckle, "John Nicholson."

74. Coleman, *Transformation of Rhode Island*, p. 73.

75. Nathan Rosenberg, "Factors Affecting the Diffusion of Technology," p. 19.

76. Habakkuk, *American and British Technology*, p. 188.

77. Lindstrom, *Economic Development in the Philadelphia Region*, pp. 9ff.

78. Quoted in John E. Kasson, *Civilizing the Machine*, pp. 24–25.

5. Industrial Upsurge, 1825–40

1. Paul Penrose Christiansen, "Land, Labor and Mechanization," p. 276; Hunter, *History of Industrial Power*, 1:516–28.

2. Lindstrom, *Economic Development in the Philadelphia Region*, p. 48.

3. Sidney Pollard, *The Genesis of Modern Management*, p. 80.

4. For discussion of the economic value of railroads and canals, see Robert

William Fogel, *Railroads and American Economic Growth*; and Carter Goodrich et al., *Canals and American Economic Development*, pp. 226ff.

5. Archibald Douglas Turnbull, *John Stevens*, pp. 362–66. For further discussion of the value of canals, see Lindstrom, *Economic Development in the Philadelphia Region*, pp. 112–19; and Julius Rubin, *Canal or Railroad?*.

6. Diane Lindstrom, "Demand, Markets and Economic Development: Philadelphia, 1815–1840," p. 271. For imports and exports, see Jeffrey G. Williamson, *American Economic Growth and the Balance of Payments, 1820–1913*.

7. Peter Temin, *The Jacksonian Economy*, pp. 154–55.

8. These fluctuations are still best discussed in F. W. Taussig, *The Tariff History of the United States*.

9. Bishop, *History of American Manufactures*, 2:378.

10. French, *Rise and Progress of the Iron Trade*, pp. 54–55.

11. Elva Tooker, *Nathan Trotter, Philadelphia Merchant*, pp. 91–95.

12. Clark claims, however, that no state government action permanently assisted manufacturing before 1860. *History of Manufactures*, 1:265.

13. Temin says that the BUS could have helped but did not. *Jacksonian Economy*, p. 55.

14. Sylla, "American Banking and Growth," pp. 219–24.

15. Temin, *Jacksonian Economy*, pp. 162.

16. Ibid., pp. 105–20.

17. Stephanie Grauman Wolf, *An Urban Village*.

18. Hurbert G. Schmidt, *Rural Hunterdon*, pp. 77–79.

19. Percy Wells Bidwell and John I. Falconer, *History of Agriculture in the Northern United States, 1620–1860*, p. 204.

20. Earle and Hoffman, "Commerce and Labor," pp. 44–45.

21. Clark, *History of Manufactures*, 1:393.

22. Clarence H. Danhof, *Change in Agriculture*, p. 268.

23. Bidwell and Falconer, *Agriculture in the Northern United States*, p. 196.

24. Danhof, *Change in Agriculture*, p. 11.

25. Paul W. Gates reports that the census of 1821 showed 106,000 freeholders and 80,000 tenants in New York State. *The Farmer's Age*, p. 36.

26. Robert Doherty, *Society and Power*, p. 21.

27. Schmidt, *Rural Hunterdon*, pp. 80–87.

28. Danhof, *Change in Agriculture*, p. 252.

29. Gates, *Farmer's Age*, pp. 232–33.

30. Danhof, *Change in Agriculture*, p. 188.

31. Bidwell and Falconer, *Agriculture in the Northern United States*, p. 214; Danhof, *Change in Agriculture*, pp. 219–20.

32. Danhof, *Change in Agriculture*, pp. 206, 256; Schmidt, *Rural Hunterdon*, pp. 102–7.

33. Richard A. Easterlin, "Population Change and Farm Settlement in the Northern United States," pp. 45–46.

34. Tryon, *Household Manufactures*, pp. 190–202.

35. Bidwell and Falconer, *Agriculture in the Northern United States*, p. 251.

36. Arthur Harrison Cole, *The American Wool Manufacture*, 1:91.
37. Everett Edwards, "American Agriculture," p. 207.
38. Lindstrom, *Economic Development in the Philadelphia Region*, p. 12.
39. Diane Lindstrom and John Sharpless, "Urban Growth and Economic Structure in Antebellum America," pp. 165–77.
40. Bishop, *History of American Manufactures*, 2:363.
41. Ibid., 2:263–64.
42. Lindstrom, *Economic Development in the Philadelphia Region*, pp. 5ff.
43. Pred, *Urban Growth*, p. 109. See also Roger L. Ransom, "Interregional Canals and Economic Specialization in the Antebellum United States," pp. 13–27.
44. Phyllis Deane, *The First Industrial Revolution*, p. 76.
45. Baldwin Locomotive Company records, Eleutherian Mills Historical Library, Greenville, Del.
46. French, *Rise and Progress of the Iron Trade*, p. 54. Jacob Bigelow, the first Rumford Professor of Science at Harvard, wrote in 1831 of charcoal and coke smelting without discussing the superiority of either. *Elements of Technology*, pp. 280ff. See also Richard H. Schallenberg and David A. Ault, "Raw Materials Supply and Technological Change in the American Charcoal Iron Industry," p. 437.
47. Mark Richards's rolling and nail mill in Manayunk, Pennsylvania, had 636 employees in 1828. *History of American Manufactures*, 2:326–27.
48. For the early history of iron processing in the United States, see W. Paul Strassman, *Risk and Technological Innovation*, pp. 24–26.
49. Bishop, *History of American Manufactures*, 2:303.
50. For a history of the Franklin Institute's activities, see Bruce Sinclair, *Philadelphia's Philosopher Mechanics*.
51. Gibb, *Saco-Lowell Shops*; Anthony F. C. Wallace, *Rockdale*, pp. 152–57.
52. Oliver, *History of American Technology*, p. 200.
53. Ibid., pp. 185–87.
54. Thomas C. Cochran and Reuben Reina, *Entrepreneurship in Argentine Culture*, pp. 94–97.
55. Sellers, *Early Engineering Reminiscences*, pp. 112, 126.
56. Bishop, *History of American Manufactures*, 2:363.
57. Coleman, *Transformation of Rhode Island*, p. 109.
58. Clark, *History of Manufactures*, 1:516.
59. Gene Cesari, "Technology in the American Arms Industry, 1790–1860."
60. Robert S. Woodbury, "The Legend of Eli Whitney and Interchangeable Parts," p. 251.
61. Clark, *History of Manufactures*, 1:543ff., 447.
62. Coleman, *Transformation of Rhode Island*, p. 97.
63. Melvin Thomas Copeland, *The Cotton Manufacturing Industry of the United States*, pp. 10ff.; Clark, *History of Manufactures*, 1:549; Wallace, *Rockdale*, p. 198.
64. Diane Lindstrom, "Demand, Markets and Economic Development: The Greater Philadelphia Region," p. 30.

65. Deane, *First Industrial Revolution*, p. 51; Mathias, *First Industrial Nation*, p. 18. Mathias lists many other factors.
66. Lindstrom, *Economic Development in the Philadelphia Region*, pp. 9ff.
67. Deane, *First Industrial Revolution*, p. 77.
68. For American debates about railroads, see Rubin, *Canal or Railroad?* The French parliament sent a commission to study American railroads in 1838.

6. Industrial Maturity, 1840–55

1. Lindstrom, *Economic Development in the Philadelphia Region*, p. 154; Nathan Rosenberg, ed. *The American System of Manufactures*, p. 3.
2. Mathias, *First Industrial Nation*, pp. 278–79. See also W. R. Lawson, *British Railways*.
3. John Stevens, *Documents Tending To Prove the Superior Advantages of Rail-Ways and Steam Carriages over Canal Navigation*, p. 2; see also the preface by Arthur H. Cole.
4. Thomas P. Hughes, "A Technological Frontier," p. 57. For excellent brief analyses of American culture as exemplified in industry, see John E. Sawyer, "The Social Basis of the American System of Manufacturing," pp. 361–79; and Hugo A. Meier, "The Ideology of Technology," pp. 79–97.
5. For the best discussion of the impact of railroads, see Albert Fishlow, *American Railroads and the Transformation of the Antebellum Economy*.
6. The Albany and Schenectady, the Baltimore and Ohio, and the Charleston and Hamburg had completed sections of track as early as 1830, but none of them made a major through passage to an interior system.
7. Paul H. Cootner, "The Economic Impact of the Railroad Innovation," pp. 108–9.
8. Frederick A. Cleveland and Fred Wilbur Powell, *Railroad Finance*.
9. Richard B. Du Boff, "Business Demand and the Development of the Telegraph in the United States, 1844–1860."
10. Glenn Porter and Harold C. Livesay, *Merchants and Manufacturers*, p. 80.
11. Fishlow, *American Railroads*, p. 123.
12. James M. Swank, *History of the Manufacture of Iron in All Ages*, pp. 339–47.
13. Peter Temin, *Iron and Steel in Nineteenth-Century America*, p. 52.
14. Rosenberg, *American System of Manufactures*, p. 267.
15. The demands of the railroads greatly expanded the iron industry around Baltimore. Brown, *Baltimore in the Nation*, p. 223.
16. Swank, *Manufacture of Iron*, pp. 343–50.
17. W. David Lewis, "The Early History of the Lackawanna Iron and Coal Company," pp. 427–64.
18. For detailed analysis, see Temin, *Iron and Steel*, pp. 51–80.
19. John Anderson, quoted in Rosenberg, *American System of Manufactures*, p. 66.

20. Robert C. Allen, "The Peculiar Productivity History of American Blast Furnaces, 1840–1913," pp. 628–29.
21. Tyler, *American Clyde*, pp. 3–4.
22. Ibid.
23. Oliver, *History of American Technology*, p. 203.
24. Copeland, *Cotton Manufacturing Industry*, p. 9.
25. Coleman, *Transformation of Rhode Island*, p. 132.
26. Clark, *History of Manufactures*, 1:550–57.
27. Hunter, *History of Industrial Power*, 1:300–44.
28. Bishop, *History of American Manufactures*, 2:401.
29. Edwin T. Freedley, *Leading Pursuits and Leading Men*, pp. 335–38.
30. Clark, *History of Manufactures*, 1:518.
31. Freedley, *Leading Pursuits and Leading Men*, pp. 329–30.
32. The unreliability of statistics for 1850 makes exact figures useless, but the rank orders appear to be beyond doubt.
33. James E. Riggs, *New York Becomes the Empire State*, pp. 337–40.
34. Daniel Hodas, *The Business Career of Moses Taylor*, pp. 80–100.
35. Paul Uselding, "Technical Progress at the Springfield Armory, 1820–1850," pp. 292, 306.
36. Eighth Census of the United States, cited in Gates, *Farmer's Age*, p. 291.
37. In his introduction to a recent edition of the report, Rosenberg questions the meaning of "maturity" as an economic term but agrees as to the advanced position of the United States. *American System of Manufactures*, p. 2n.
38. Sawyer, "Social Basis of the American System, pp. 370–71.
39. Rosenberg, *American System of Manufactures*, pp. 193–95.

7. The Evolving Business System

1. Lindstrom, "Demand, Markets and Economic Development: Philadelphia, 1815–1840," p. 271.
2. Porter and Livesay, *Merchants and Manufacturers*, p. 20.
3. James D. Norris, *R. G. Dun & Co., 1841–1900*, pp. 9, 10–35.
4. A report on prices at auction sales was published in Philadelphia from 1812 to 1827. See David P. Forsyth, *The Business Press in America, 1750–1865*, p. 56.
5. Ibid., pp. 63–98.
6. Arthur Harrison Cole, *The Historical Development of Economics and Business Literature*," pp. 24–42.
7. Sinclair, *Philadelphia's Philosopher Mechanics*, pp. 7–8; quotation from p. 89.
8. Wallace, *Rockdale*, pp. 229–37.
9. Sinclair, *Philadelphia's Philosopher Mechanics*, p. ix; Wallace, *Rockdale*, p. 231.
10. Quoted in E. G. Dexter, *History of Education in the United States*, p. 346.

11. Robert E. Carlson, "British Railroads and Engineers and the Beginning of American Railway Development," pp. 139–41.
12. Evans, *Business Incorporations.*
13. Thomas C. Cochran, *200 Years of American Business*, pp. 76–77.
14. For more discussion, see Thomas C. Cochran, *Business in American Life*, pp. 114–22.
15. Davis, *Earlier History of American Corporations*, 1:294.
16. Sellers, *Early Engineering Reminiscences*, pp. 46–49.
17. Wallace, *Rockdale*, pp. 387–88.
18. Porter and Livesay, *Merchants and Manufacturers*, p. 116.
19. Alfred D. Chandler, *The Visible Hand*, pp. 81ff.
20. Quoted in Thomas C. Cochran, *Railroad Leaders, 1845–1890*, p. 37.
21. Thomas C. Cochran, introduction to Charles Francis Adams, Jr., *Railroads*, pp. xxiv–xxv.
22. Alfred D. Chandler, *Henry Varnum Poor*, pp. 164–66; quotation from p. 155.
23. Cochran, *Railroad Leaders*, pp. 109–25.
24. Thomas Hamilton, *Men and Manners in America*, p. 74.

8. Industrial Society

1. Coleman, *Transformation of Rhode Island*, p. 229; quotation from p. 73.
2. Henry Wansey, *Henry Wansey and His American Journal, 1794*, p. 134.
3. Harold Hancock, "The Industrial Worker along the Brandywine, 1800–1830," p. 1.
4. Wallace, *Rockdale*, p. 314.
5. Marcus L. Hansen, *The Atlantic Migration, 1607–1860*, pp. 69–97; quotation from p. 68.
6. Herbert Heaton, "The Industrial Immigrant in the United States, 1783–1812," pp. 519–22.
7. These figures are from federal records. See William J. Bromwell, *History of Immigration to the United States.*
8. Stanley Lebergott, *Manpower in Economic Growth*, p. 77.
9. Donald R. Adams, Jr. "Wage Rates in the Early National Period," p. 420. Lebergott does not find real wage and national income trends necessarily related. *Manpower in Economic Growth*, p. 140.
10. Adams "Wage Rates," p. 406.
11. Lebergott, *Manpower in Economic Growth*, p. 115.
12. Adams, "Wage Rates," pp. 424–25.
13. Ware, *Early New England Cotton Manufacture*, pp. 238–45.
14. Lozier, "Forgotten Industry."
15. Hancock, "Industrial Worker along the Brandywine," pp. 39–43; Wallace, *Rockdale*, pp. 61–63, 171–78.
16. Coleman, *Transformation of Rhode Island*, p. 233.
17. Wallace, *Rockdale*, p. 178.
18. Rosenberg, "Anglo-American Wage Differentials," pp. 221–29.

19. Jeffrey G. Williamson, "American Prices and Urban Inequality since 1820," p. 313, 313n. Williamson cites Lebergott's figures.
20. Richard A. McLeod, "The Philadelphia Artisan, 1820–1850," pp. 2–21.
21. Herbert G. Gutman, "Work, Culture, and Society in Industrial America, 1815–1919."
22. Dorothy S. Brady, "Consumption and the Style of Life," p. 68.
23. Wallace, *Rockdale*, pp. 63–64. There is no reason to suppose that Rockdale was atypical. See Ware, *Early New England Cotton Manufacture*, p. 280.
24. Wallace, *Rockdale*, pp. 59–61.
25. Ibid., p. 65; quotation from p. 59. See pp. 62–63 for an estimated annual budget.
26. Coleman, *Transformation of Rhode Island*, p. 233; Ware, *Early New England Cotton Manufacture*, pp. 244–48; Hancock, "Industrial Worker along the Brandywine," pp. 34–35.
27. Analysis of some Middle States county records indicates a continuous turnover in tenants that made profit minimal to the owner, who gained eventually only from the increasing value of land.
28. Hancock, "Industrial Worker along the Brandywine," pp. 37, 129–31.
29. Sam B. Warner, *The Private City*.
30. Hancock, "Industrial Worker along the Brandywine," p. 81.
31. Coleman, *Transformation of Rhode Island*, p. 244; Ware, *Early New England Cotton Manufacture*, p. 268.
32. For more discussion, see Cochran, *Business in American Life*, pp. 117–21.
33. Ellwood P. Cubberly, *Public Education in the United States*, p. 51.
34. Newton Edwards and Herman G. Richey, *The School in the American Social Order*, p. 273; quotation from p. 247.
35. For more detail, see Cochran, *Business in American Life*, pp. 91–102.
36. Quoted in Merle E. Curti, *The Social Ideas of American Educators*, p. 12.
37. Ibid., p. 97.
38. Seymour Lipset, *The First New Nation*, p. 118.
39. Perry Miller, *American Character*, p. 23.
40. H. G. Barnett, *Innovation*, pp. 87–89.
41. Robert R. Palmer, "Ideas That Did Not Migrate to America," p. 370.

Bibliography

Adams, Charles Francis, Jr. *Railroads: Their Origin and Problems.* 1887. Reprint. Introduced by Thomas C. Cochran. New York: Harper & Row, 1969.

Adams, Donald R., Jr. *Finance and Enterprise in Early America: A Study of Stephen Girard's Bank.* Philadelphia: University of Pennsylvania Press, 1979.

————. "The Mid-Atlantic Labor Market in the Early Nineteenth Century." In *Business and Economic History: Papers Presented at the Twenty-Fourth Annual Meeting of the Business History Conference,* edited by Paul Uselding. 2d ser., vol. 7. Urbana: Bureau of Economic and Business Research, 1979.

————. "Some Evidence on English and American Wage Rates." *Journal of Economic History* 30 (September 1970).

————. "Wage Rates in the Early National Period." *Journal of Economic History* 28 (September 1968).

Albion, Robert G. *The Rise of New York Port, 1815–1860.* New York: Scribner's, 1939.

Allen, Robert C. "The Peculiar Productivity History of American Blast Furnaces, 1840–1913." *Journal of Economic History* 37 (September 1977).

Arbuckle, Robert D. "John Nicholson and the Attempt to Promote Pennsylvania Manufacturing." *Pennsylvania History* 42 (April 1975).

Ashton, Thomas S. *Iron and Steel in the Industrial Revolution.* Manchester, England: Manchester University Press, 1924.

Atack, Jeremy. "Returns to Scale in Antebellum United States Manufacturing." *Explorations in Economic History* 14 (October 1977).

Bagehot, Walter. *Lombard Street: A Description of the Money Market.* New York: Scribner's, 1873.

Bagnall, William R. *The Textile Industries of the United States.* Vol. 1, *1639–1810.* Cambridge: Riverside Press, 1893.

Bailis, Stanley. "The Development and Significance of Role-Modification Directives under Rapid Socio-Cultural Change." Ph.D. dissertation, University of Pennsylvania, 1971.

159

Barnett, H. G. *Innovation: The Basis of Cultural Change*. New York: McGraw-Hill, 1950.

Barrett, William. *Time of Need: Forms of Imagination in the Twentieth Century*. New York: Harper & Row, Torchbooks, 1972.

Batchelder, Samuel. *Introduction and Early Progress of the Cotton Manufacture in the United States*. Boston: Little, Brown, 1863.

Bathe, Greville, and Dorothy Bathe. *Oliver Evans: A Chronicle of Early American Engineering*. Philadelphia: Historical Society of Pennsylvania, 1935.

Berthoff, Rowland Tappan. *British Immigrants in Industrial America, 1790–1950*. Cambridge: Harvard University Press, 1951.

Bidwell, Percy Wells, and John I. Falconer. *History of Agriculture in the Northern United States, 1620–1860*. 1925. Reprint. New York: Peter Smith, 1941.

Bigelow, Jacob, M. D. *Elements of Technology*. Boston: Hilliard, Gray, Little and Wilkins, 1831.

Binder, Frederick Moore. *Coal Age Empire: Pennsylvania Coal and Its Utilization to 1860*. Harrisburg: Pennsylvania Historical and Museum Commission, 1974.

Bining, Arthur Cecil. *Pennsylvania Iron Manufacture in the Eighteenth Century*. 2d ed. Harrisburg: Pennsylvania Historical and Museum Commission, 1973.

Bishop, John Leander. *A History of American Manufactures from 1608 to 1860*. 2 vols. Philadelphia: Edward Young, 1864.

Bjork, Gordon C. "Foreign Trade." In *The Growth of the Seaport Cities, 1790–1825*, edited by David T. Gilchrist. Charlottesville: University Press of Virginia, for the Eleutherian Mills–Hagley Foundation, 1967.

Blouin, Francis X., Jr. "The Boston Region, 1810–1850: A Study of Urbanization on a Regional Scale." Ph.D. dissertation, University of Minnesota, 1978.

Boatman, Roy M. "The Brandywine Cotton Industry, 1795–1865." Hagley Museum Research Report. Greenville, Del.: Eleutherian Mills Historical Library, 1955.

Bolles, Albert S. *Industrial History of the United States, from the Earliest Settlements to the Present Time*. Norwich, Conn.: Henry Bill, 1878.

Brady, Dorothy S. "Consumption and the Style of Life." In *American Economic Growth: An Economist's History of the United States*, edited by Lance E. Davis, Richard A. Easterlin, and William N. Parker. New York: Harper & Row, 1972.

———. "Trade and Manufactures." In *The Growth of the Seaport Cities, 1790–1825*, edited by David T. Gilchrist. Charlottesville: University Press of Virginia, for the Eleutherian Mills–Hagley Foundation, 1967.

Brewer, Thomas B. "The Formative Period of 140 American Manufacturing Companies, 1789–1929." Ph.D. dissertation, University of Pennsylvania, 1962.

Brewington, Marion V. "Maritime Philadelphia, 1609–1837." *Pennsylvania Magazine of History and Biography* 63 (April 1939).

Bromwell, William J. *History of Immigration to the United States (From Official Data)*. New York: Redfield, 1856.

Brown, Gary Lawson. *Baltimore in the Nation, 1789–1861.* Chapel Hill: University of North Carolina Press, 1980.

Bruchey, Stuart. "The Business Economy of Marketing Change, 1790–1840: A Study in Sources of Efficiency." *Agricultural History* 41 (January 1972).

———. *Robert Oliver, Merchant of Baltimore, 1783–1819.* Baltimore: Johns Hopkins University Press, 1956.

Buell, Augustus C. *The Memoirs of Charles H. Cramp.* Philadelphia: Lippincott, 1906.

Carlson, Robert E. "British Railroads and Engineers and the Beginning of American Railway Development." *Business History Review* 34 (Summer 1960).

Carlton, Frank Tracy. *Economic Influences upon Educational Progress in the United States.* 1908. Reprint. New York: Teachers College Press, 1965.

Carossa, Vincent. *Investment Banking in America: A History.* Cambridge: Harvard University Press, 1970.

Cesari, Gene. "Technology in the American Arms Industry, 1790–1860." Ph.D. dissertation, University of Pennsylvania, 1970.

Chandler, Alfred D. *Henry Varnum Poor: Business Editor, Analyst and Reformer.* Cambridge: Harvard University Press, 1956.

———. "Henry Varnum Poor: Philosopher of Management." In *Men in Business: Essays in the History of Entrepreneurship,* edited by William Miller. Cambridge: Harvard University Press, 1952.

———. *The Visible Hand: The Managerial Revolution in American Business.* Cambridge: Harvard University Press, 1977.

Chapman, Stanley D. "British Marketing Enterprise: The Changing Roles of Merchants, Manufacturers, and Financiers, 1700–1860." *Business History Review* 53 (Summer 1979).

———. "The Textile Factory before Arkwright: A Typology of Factory Development." *Business History Review* 48 (Winter 1974).

Christensen, Paul Penrose. "Land, Labor and Mechanization." Ph.D. dissertation, University of Wisconsin, 1976.

Clark, Victor S. *History of Manufactures in the United States, 1607–1860.* Vol. 1. New York: McGraw-Hill, 1929.

Cleveland, Frederick A., and Fred Wilbur Powell. *Railroad Finance.* New York: Appleton, 1923.

Cochran, Thomas C. *Business in American Life: A History.* New York: McGraw-Hill, 1972.

———. "The Business Revolution." *American Historical Review* 79 (December 1974).

———. *Pennsylvania: A Bicentennial History.* New York: Norton, 1978.

———. *Railroad Leaders, 1845–1890: The Business Mind in Action.* Cambridge: Harvard University Press, 1953.

———. *200 Years of American Business.* New York: Basic Books, 1977.

———, and Reuben Reina. *Entrepreneurship in Argentine Culture.* Philadelphia: University of Pennsylvania Press, 1962.

Cohen, Ira. "The Auction System in the Port of New York." *Business History Review* 45 (Winter 1971).

Cole, Arthur Harrison. *The American Wool Manufacture.* 2 vols. Cambridge: Harvard University Press, 1926.

———. *The Historical Development of Economics and Business Literature.* Kress Library Publication 12. Boston: Harvard School of Business Administration, 1957.

———, and Harold F. Williamson. *The American Carpet Manufacture.* Cambridge; Harvard University Press, 1941.

Coleman, Peter J. *Debtors and Creditors in America: Insolvency, Imprisonment for Debt, and Bankruptcy, 1607–1900.* Madison: State Historical Society of Wisconsin, 1974.

———. *The Transformation of Rhode Island, 1790–1860.* Providence: Brown University Press, 1963.

Condit, Carl W. *American Building.* Chicago: University of Chicago Press, 1968.

Cooke, Jacob E. *Tench Coxe and the Early Republic.* Chapel Hill: University of North Carolina Press, 1978.

Cootner, Paul H. "The Economic Impact of the Railroad Innovation." In *The Railroad and the Space Program: An Exploration in Historical Analogy,* edited by Bruce Mazlish. Cambridge: MIT Press, 1965.

Copeland, Melvin Thomas. *The Cotton Manufacturing Industry of the United States.* Cambridge: Harvard University Press, 1917.

[Coxe, Tench?]. *Observations on the Agriculture, Manufactures, and Commerce of the United States.* New York, 1789.

———. *A Statement of the Arts and Manufactures of the United States of America for the Year 1810.* Philadelphia: Cornman, 1814.

Cubberly, Ellwood P. *Public Education in the United States.* Boston: Houghton Mifflin, 1919.

Cudd, John M. *The Chicopee Manufacturing Company, 1823–1915.* Wilmington: Scholarly Resources, 1974.

Curti, Merle E. *The Social Ideas of American Educators.* New York: Scribner's, 1935.

Danhof, Clarence H. *Change in Agriculture: The Northern United States, 1820–1870.* Cambridge: Harvard University Press, 1969.

David, Paul A. "New Light on a Statistical Dark Age: U.S. Real Product Growth before 1840." *American Economic Review* 57 (1967). Reprinted in *The New Economic History,* edited by Peter Temin. New York: Penguin, 1973.

———. *Technical Choice, Innovation and Economic Growth: Essays on British and American Experience in the Nineteenth Century.* Cambridge, England: At the University Press, 1975.

Davis, Joseph Stancliffe. *Essays in the Earlier History of American Corporations.* 2 vols. Cambridge: Harvard University Press, 1917.

Davis, Lance E., Richard A. Easterlin, and William N. Parker, eds. *American Economic Growth: An Economist's History of the United States.* New York: Harper & Row, 1972.

———, and Peter L. Payne. "From Benevolence to Business: The Story of Two Savings Banks." *Business History Review* 32 (Winter 1958).

Davis, Pearce. *The Development of the American Glass Industry*. Cambridge: Harvard University Press, 1949.

Deane, Phyllis. *The First Industrial Revolution*. Cambridge, England: At the University Press, 1965.

Dexter, E. G. *History of Education in the United States*. New York: Macmillan, 1922.

Deyrup, Felicia Johnson. *Arms Makers of the Connecticut Valley: A Regional Study of the Economic Development of the Small Arms Industry, 1798–1870*. Smith College Studies in History 33. Northampton, Mass.: Smith College, 1948.

Dickinson, H. W. *A Short History of the Steam Engine*. Cambridge, England: At the University Press, 1938.

Doherty, Robert. *Society and Power: Five New England Towns, 1800–1860*. Amherst: University of Massachusetts Press, 1977.

Domett, Henry W. *A History of the Bank of New York, 1784–1884*. New York: Putnam's Sons, 1884.

Douglass, Elisha P. *The Coming of Age of American Business: Three Centuries of Enterprise, 1600–1900*. Chapel Hill: University of North Carolina Press, 1971.

Du Boff, Richard B. "Business Demand and the Development of the Telegraph in the United States, 1844–1860." *Business History Review* 54 (Winter 1980).

Earle, Carville V., and Ronald A. Hoffman. "Commerce and Labor: Urbanization and Industrialization in Antebellum America." Seminar paper, July 19, 1978, Regional Economic History Research Center, Eleutherian Mills–Hagley Foundation, Greenville, Del.

Easterlin, Richard A. "Population Change and Farm Settlement in the Northern United States." *Journal of Economic History* 36 (March 1976).

Edwards, Everett. "American Agriculture: The First 300 Years." In *United States Department of Agriculture Yearbook, 1940*. Washington, D.C.: Government Printing Office, n.d.

Edwards, Newton, and Herman G. Richey. *The School in the American Social Order: The Dynamics of Education*. Boston: Houghton Mifflin, 1947.

Ellis, David M., et al. *A Short History of New York State*. Ithaca: Cornell University Press and New York Historical Association, 1957.

Engerman, Stanley L. "Douglas C. North's *The Economic Growth of the United States, 1790–1860* Revisited." *Social Science History* 1 (Winter 1977).

Evans, George Heberton, Jr. *Business Incorporations in the United States, 1800–1943*. New York: National Bureau of Economic Research, 1948.

Fenstermaker, J. Van. *The Development of American Commercial Banking, 1782–1837*. Kent State University Bureau of Economic and Business Research 5. Kent, Ohio: Bureau of Economic and Business Research, 1965.

Ferguson, Eugene S. *The Americanness of American Technology*. Wilmington: Eleutherian Mills–Hagley Foundation, 1975.

———. *The Critical Period in American Technology*. Wilmington: Eleutherian Mills–Hagley Foundation, 1965.

——. *Oliver Evans*. Wilmington: Eleutherian Mills–Hagley Foundation, 1977.

——. "Technology as Knowledge." In *Technology and Social Change in America*, edited by Edwin T. Layton, Jr. New York: Harper & Row, 1973.

——, ed. *Early Engineering Reminiscences (1815–40) of George Escol Sellers*. Washington, D.C.: Smithsonian Institution, 1965.

Fishbein, Meyer H. "Business History Resources in the National Archives." *Business History Review* 38 (Summer 1964).

——. "The Census of Manufactures, 1810–90." National Archives Accessions 57, June 1963, supplement to *National Archives Guide*.

Fishlow, Albert. *American Railroads and the Transformation of the Antebellum Economy*. Cambridge: Harvard University Press, 1965.

Fitch, John. *Autobiography of John Fitch*. Edited by Frank D. Prager. Philadelphia: American Philosophical Society, 1976.

Flick, Alexander C., ed. *History of the State of New York*. 10 vols. New York: Columbia University Press, 1934.

Fogel, Robert William. *Railroads and American Economic Growth: Essays in Economic History*. Baltimore: Johns Hopkins University Press, 1964.

——, and Stanley L. Engerman, eds. *The Reinterpretation of American Economic History*. New York: Harper & Row, 1971.

Folsom, Burton W., II. "Urban Networks: The Economic and Social Order of the Lackawanna and Lehigh Valleys during Early Industrialization, 1850–1880." Ph.D. dissertation, University of Pittsburgh, 1976.

Forsyth, David P. *The Business Press in America, 1750–1865*. Philadelphia: Chilton, 1964.

Foulke, Roy F. *Sinews of American Commerce*. New York: Dun & Bradstreet, 1941.

Freedley, Edwin T. *Leading Pursuits and Leading Men*. Philadelphia: Lippincott, 1854.

French, B. F. *History of the Rise and Progress of the Iron Trade of the United States from 1621 to 1857*. New York: Wiley & Halstead, 1858.

Freyer, Tony A. *Forums of Order: Federal Courts and Business in American History*. Greenwich, Conn.: JAI Press, 1979.

Gallman, Robert E., ed. *Recent Developments in the Study of Business and Economic History: Essays in Memory of Herman E. Krooss*. Greenwich, Conn.: JAI Press, 1977.

Garber, John Palmer. *The Valley of the Delaware and Its Place in American History*. Philadelphia: John Winston, 1934.

Gates, Paul W. *The Farmer's Age: Agriculture, 1815–1860*. New York: Holt, Reinhart, Winston, 1960.

Gibb, George S. "The Pre-Industrial Revolution in America: A Field for Local Research." *Bulletin of the Business History Society* 20 (October 1946).

——. *The Saco-Lowell Shops: Textile Machinery Building in New England*. Cambridge: Harvard University Press, 1950.

Gilchrist, David T., ed. *The Growth of the Seaport Cities, 1790–1825*. Charlottesville: University Press of Virginia, for the Eleutherian Mills–Hagley Foundation, 1967.

Gilfillan, S. Colum. *The Sociology of Invention*. Chicago: Follett, 1935.

Goodrich, Carter, et al. *Canals and American Economic Development*. New York: Columbia University Press, 1961.

Gras, N. S. B. *The Massachusetts First National Bank of Boston, 1784–1934*. Cambridge: Harvard University Press, 1937.

Greef, Albert O. *The Commercial Paper House in the United States*. Cambridge: Harvard University Press, 1938.

Gregg, Dorothy. "John Stevens, General Entrepreneur, 1749–1838." In *Men in Business: Essays in the History of Entrepreneurship*, edited by William Miller. Cambridge: Harvard University Press, 1952.

Griffin, Richard W. "An Origin of the Industrial Revolution in Maryland: The Textile Industry, 1789–1826." *Maryland Historical Magazine* 61 (March 1966).

Gutman, Herbert G. "Work, Culture, and Society in Industrial America, 1815–1919." *American Historical Review* 78 (June 1973).

Habakkuk, H. J. *American and British Technology in the Nineteenth Century: The Search for Labour-Saving Inventions*. Cambridge, England: At the University Press, 1962.

Hagnar, Charles V. *Early History of the Falls of the Schuylkill, Manayunk, Schuylkill and Lehigh Navigation Companies*. Philadelphia: Claxton, 1869.

Hamilton, Thomas. *Men and Manners in America*. Edinburgh, Scotland: Blackwood, 1843.

Hammond, Bray. *Banks and Politics in America from the Revolution to the Civil War*. Princeton: Princeton University Press, 1957.

Hancock, Harold. "Delaware Papermakers and Papermaking, 1787–1840." Hagley Museum Research Report. Greenville, Del.: Eleutherian Mills Historical Library, 1955.

———. "The Industrial Worker along the Brandywine, 1800–1830." Hagley Museum Research Report. Greenville, Del.: Eleutherian Mills Historical Library, 1956.

Handlin, Oscar, and Mary Flug Handlin. *Commonwealth: A Study of the Role of Government in the American Economy, Massachusetts, 1774–1861*. New York: New York University Press, 1947.

Hansen, Marcus L. *The Atlantic Migration, 1607–1860*. Cambridge: Harvard University Press, 1951.

Hardie, James. *The Description of the City of New York*. New York: Samuel Marks, 1827.

Hareven, Tamara K., ed. *Family and Kin in Urban Communities, 1700–1930*. New York: Franklin Watts, 1977.

Harris, J. R. *Industry and Technology in the Eighteenth Century: Britain and France*. Birmingham, England: University of Birmingham, 1972.

Hartz, Louis. *Economic Policy and Democratic Thought: Pennsylvania, 1776–1860*. Cambridge: Harvard University Press, 1948.

Heaton, Herbert. "The Industrial Immigrant in the United States, 1783–1812." *Proceedings of the American Philosophical Society* 95 (1951).

Hedges, James B. *The Browns of Providence Plantation: The Nineteenth Century*. Providence: Brown University Press, 1968.

Higgins, J. P., and Sidney Pollard, eds. *Aspects of Capital Investment in Great Britain, 1750–1850*. London: Methuen, 1971.

Hindle, Brooke, ed. *America's Wooden Age: Aspects of Its Early Technology*. North Tarrytown, N.Y.: Sleepy Hollow Restorations, 1975.

Hodas, Daniel. *The Business Career of Moses Taylor: Merchant, Finance Capitalist, and Industrialist*. New York: New York University Press, 1976.

―――. "Report on Research Possibilities at Eleutherian Mills Library." Greenville, Del.: Eleutherian Mills Historical Library, 1974.

Holmes, Graeme M. *Britain and America: A Comparative Economic History*. New York: Barnes & Noble, 1976.

Holmes, Will. "Early American Sawmills." Hagley Museum Research Report. Greenville, Del.: Eleutherian Mills Historical Library, 1960.

Horwitz, Morton J. *The Transformation of American Law, 1780–1860*. Cambridge: Harvard University Press, 1977.

Hughes, Jonathan. *Industrialization and Economic History: Thesis and Conjectures*. New York: McGraw-Hill, 1970.

Hughes, Thomas P. "A Technological Frontier." In *The Railroad and the Space Program: An Exploration in Historical Analogy*, edited by Bruce Mazlish. Cambridge: MIT Press, 1965.

Hunter, Dard. *Papermaking in Pioneer America*. Philadelphia: University of Pennsylvania Press, 1952.

Hunter, Louis C. "The Heroic Theory of Invention." In *Technology and Social Change in America*, edited by Edwin T. Layton, Jr. New York: Harper & Row, 1973.

―――. *A History of Industrial Power in the United States, 1780–1930*. Vol. 1, *Waterpower in the Century of the Steam Engine*. Charlottesville: University Press of Virginia, for the Eleutherian Mills–Hagley Foundation, 1979.

―――. *Steamboats on the Western Rivers*. Cambridge: Harvard University Press, 1949.

Hussey, Miriam. *From Merchants to "Colour Men": Five Generations of Samuel Wetherill's White Lead Business*. Philadelphia: University of Pennsylvania Press, 1956.

Jeremy, David John. "British Textile Technology Transition to the United States: The Philadelphia Region's Experience, 1770–1820." *Business History Review* 47 (Spring 1973).

―――. "The Transmission of Cotton and Woollen Manufacturing Technologies between Britain and the United States of America from 1790 to the 1830s." Ph.D. dissertation, London School of Economics and Political Science, University of London, 1978.

―――, ed. *Henry Wansey and His American Journal, 1794*. Philadelphia: American Philosophical Society, 1970.

Kaestle, Carl F., and Maris A. Vinovskis. *Education and Social Change in Nineteenth Century Massachusetts*. New York: Cambridge University Press, 1979.

Kasson, John E. *Civilizing the Machine: Technology and Republican Values in America, 1776–1900*. New York: Penguin, 1976.

Klebaner, Benjamin J. *Commercial Banking in the United States: A History.* Hinsdale, Ill.: Dryden, 1974.

Krooss, Herman. "Financial Institutions." In *The Growth of the Seaport Cities, 1790–1825*, edited by David T. Gilchrist. Charlottesville: University Press of Virginia, for the Eleutherian Mills–Hagley Foundation, 1967.

———, and Charles Gilbert. *American Business History.* Englewood Cliffs, N.J.: Prentice Hall, 1972.

Lane, Peter. *The Industrial Revolution: The Birth of the Modern Age.* New York: Barnes & Noble, 1978.

Lanier, Henry W. *A Century of Banking in New York, 1822–1922.* New York: Doran, 1922.

Laurie, Bruce. *Working People of Philadelphia, 1800–1850.* Philadelphia: Temple University Press, 1980.

Lawson, W. R. *British Railways: A Financial and Commercial Survey.* New York: Van Nostrand, 1914.

Layton, Edwin T., Jr., ed. *Technology and Social Change in America.* New York: Harper & Row, 1973.

Lebergott, Stanley. *Manpower in Economic Growth: The American Record since 1800.* New York: McGraw-Hill, 1964.

Lee, Everett S., and Michael Lalli. "Population." In *The Growth of the Seaport Cities, 1790–1825*, edited by David T. Gilchrist. Charlottesville: University Press of Virginia, for the Eleutherian Mills–Hagley Foundation, 1967.

Lee, Susan Previant, and Peter Passell. *A New Economic View of American History.* New York: Norton, 1980.

Lemon, James T. *The Best Poor Man's Country: A Geographical Study of Early Southern Pennsylvania.* Baltimore: Johns Hopkins University Press, 1972.

Lewis, Gene D. *Charles Ellet, Jr., 1810–1862: The Engineer as Individualist.* Urbana: University of Illinois Press, 1968.

Lewis, Lawrence, Jr. *A History of the Bank of North America.* Philadelphia: Lippincott, 1882.

Lewis, Ronald L. *Coal, Iron and Slaves: Industrial Slavery in Maryland and Virginia, 1715–1865.* Westport, Conn.: Greenwood, 1979.

Lewis, W. David. "The Early History of the Lackawanna Iron and Coal Company: A Study in Technological Adaptation." *Pennsylvania Magazine of History and Biography* 96 (October 1972).

———. "Iron and Steel in America: A Brief History." Hagley Museum Research Report. Greenville, Del.: Eleutherian Mills Historical Library, 1958.

Lindert, Paul H., and Jeffrey G. Williamson. "Three Centuries of American Inequality." In *Research in Economic History*, edited by Paul Uselding. Vol. 1. Greenwich, Conn.: JAI Press, 1976.

Lindstrom, Diane. "Demand, Markets and Economic Development: The Greater Philadelphia Region." Ph.D. dissertation, University of Delaware, 1974.

———. "Demand, Markets and Economic Development: Philadelphia, 1815–1840." *Journal of Economic History* 35 (March 1975).

————. *Economic Development in the Philadelphia Region, 1810–1850*. New York: Columbia University Press, 1978.

————. "The Industrialization of the North East, 1810–1860." In *Working Papers from the Regional Economic History Research Center*, edited by Glenn Porter and William H. Mulligan, Jr. Vol. 2. Greenville, Del.: Eleutherian Mills–Hagley Foundation, 1979.

————, and John Sharpless. "Urban Growth and Economic Structure in Antebellum America." In *Research in Economic History*, edited by Paul Uselding. Vol. 3. Greenwich, Conn.: JAI Press, 1979.

Lipset, Seymour. *The First New Nation: The United States in Historical and Comparative Perspective*. Garden City, N.Y.: Doubleday, Anchor, 1967.

Littleton, A. C. *Accounting Theory to 1900*. New York: American Institute Publishing Co., 1933.

Livingood, James Weston. *The Philadelphia-Baltimore Trade Rivalry, 1780–1860*. Harrisburg: Pennsylvania Historical and Museum Commission, 1947.

Lozier, John W. "The Forgotten Industry: Small and Medium Sized Cotton Mills South of Boston, 1810–1840." In *Working Papers from the Regional Economic History Research Center*, edited by Glenn Porter and William H. Mulligan, Jr. Vol. 2. Greenville, Del.: Eleutherian Mills–Hagley Foundation, 1979.

————. "Mason and Taunton." Ph.D. dissertation, Ohio State University, 1978.

Maass, Eleanor, ed. "A Public Watchdog: Thomas Pym Cope and the Philadelphia Waterworks; A Journal Edited and with an Introduction and Notes." *Proceedings of the American Philosophical Society* 124 (1980).

McLeod, Richard A. "The Philadelphia Artisan, 1828–1850." Ph.D. dissertation, University of Missouri, 1971.

Mathias, Peter. "Capital, Credit and Enterprise in the Industrial Revolution." *Journal of European Economic History* 2 (Spring 1973).

————. *The First Industrial Nation: An Economic History of Britain, 1750–1914*. New York: Scribner's, 1969.

Mazlish, Bruce, ed. *The Railroad and the Space Program: An Exploration in Historical Analogy*. Cambridge: MIT Press, 1965.

Mease, James, M.D. *The Picture of Philadelphia*. Philadelphia: T. Kite, 1811.

Meier, Hugo A. "The Ideology of Technology." In *Technology and Social Change in America*, edited by Edwin T. Layton, Jr. New York: Harper & Row, 1973.

Mesick, Jane L. *The English Traveler in America, 1785–1835*. New York: Columbia University Press, 1922.

Miller, Perry. *American Character: A Conversion*. Santa Barbara: University of California Press, 1962.

Miller, William, ed. *Men in Business: Essays in the History of Entrepreneurship*. Cambridge: Harvard University Press, 1952.

Mizushima, Sanichiro. "Background of Modernization in Japan." *Proceedings of the American Philosophical Society* 123 (1979).

Mokyr, Joel. "Demand vs. Supply in the Industrial Revolution." *Journal of Economic History* 37 (December 1977).

Morison, Elting E. *From Know-How to Nowhere.* New York: Basic Books, 1974.

Multhauf, Robert P. "America's Wooden Age." In *Building Early America: Contributions toward the History of a Great Industry,* edited by Charles E. Peterson. Radnor, Pa.: Chilton, 1976.

Myers, Margaret G. *The New York Money Market.* Vol. 1, *Origins and Development.* New York: Columbia University Press, 1931.

Nef, John U. *Cultural Foundations of Industrial Civilization.* Cambridge, England: At the University Press, 1958.

Nelson, John R., Jr. "Alexander Hamilton and American Manufacture: A Reexamination." *Journal of American History* 65 (March 1979).

New American State Papers. Vol. 1, *Manufacturing.* Wilmington: Scholarly Resources, 1972.

New York: A Guide to the Empire State. Introduction by Alfred D. Chandler, Jr. Writers' Program Work Projects Administration. New York: Oxford University Press, 1940.

New York and Philadelphia Stock Exchanges: An Historical Review. New York and Philadelphia: Historical Publishing Company, 1886.

New York State Department of Labor. *Growth of Industry in New York.* Albany: Argus, 1904.

Norris, James D. *R. G. Dun & Co., 1841–1900: The Development of Credit Reporting in the Nineteenth Century.* Westport, Conn.: Greenwood, 1978.

Oliver, John W. *History of American Technology.* New York: Ronald, 1956.

Overman, Frederick. *The Manufacture of Iron.* Philadelphia: Convention of Iron Masters, 1850.

Palmer, Robert R. "Ideas That Did Not Migrate to America." *Pennsylvania Magazine of History and Biography* 63 (April 1939).

Parker, William N. "Proto-Industrialization: A Survey of Issues." Discussion paper, December 9, 1977, Conference on Proto-Industrialism in Europe, Eleutherian Mills Historical Library, Greenville, Del.

Parsons, Burke Adrian. *British Trade Cycles and American Bank Credit: Some Aspects of Economic Fluctuations in the United States, 1815–1840.* New York: Arno, 1977.

Pessen, Edward. *Jacksonian America: Society, Personality and Politics.* Homewood, Ill.: Dorsey, 1969.

Peterson, Charles E., ed. *Building Early America: Contributions toward the History of a Great Industry.* Radnor, Pa.: Chilton, 1976.

Pitkin, Timothy. *A Statistical View of the Commerce of the United States of America.* New York: Johnson, 1967.

Pollard, Sidney. *The Genesis of Modern Management.* Cambridge: Harvard University Press, 1965.

Pomerantz, Sidney I. *New York, An American City, 1783–1803.* New York: Columbia University Press, 1938.

Porter, Glenn, and Harold C. Livesay. *Merchants and Manufacturers: Studies in the Changing Structure of Nineteenth-Century Marketing.* Baltimore: Johns Hopkins University Press, 1971.

————, and William H. Mulligan, Jr., eds. *Working Papers from the Regional Economic History Research Center.* Greenville, Del.: Eleutherian Mills–Hagley Foundation, annual, 1978–.

Poulson, Barry W. "Estimates of the Value of Manufacturing Output in the Early Nineteenth Century." *Journal of Economic History* 29 (September 1969).

Powell, H. Benjamin. "The Pennsylvania Anthracite Industry, 1769–1976." *Pennsylvania History* 47 (January 1980).

————. *Philadelphia's First Fuel Crisis: Jacob Cist and the Developing Market in Pennsylvania Anthracite.* University Park: Pennsylvania State University Press, 1978.

Pred, Allan R. *Urban Growth and the Circulation of Information: The United States System of Cities, 1790–1840.* Cambridge: Harvard University Press, 1973.

Pursell, Carroll W., Jr. *Early Stationary Steam Engines in America: A Study in the Migration of Technology.* Washington, D.C.: Smithsonian Institution, 1969.

————. "The Manufacture of Iron in the Christina-Brandywine Valley, 1720–1900." Hagley Museum Research Report. Greenville, Del.: Eleutherian Mills Historical Library, 1957.

Ransom, Roger L. "Interregional Canals and Economic Specialization in the Antebellum United States." *Explorations in Entrepreneurial History* 2d ser., 5 (Fall 1967).

Redlich, Fritz. *The Molding of American Banking: Men and Ideas.* 2 vols. New York: Hafner, 1951.

Riefler, Roger F. "Nineteenth-Century Urbanization Patterns in the United States." *Journal of Economic History* 39 (December 1979).

Riggs, James E. *New York Becomes the Empire State.* Vol. 6 of *History of the State of New York,* edited by Alexander C. Flick. New York: Columbia University Press, 1934.

Robinson, Eric H. "The Early Diffusion of Steam Power." *Journal of Economic History* 34 (March 1974).

Rock, Howard B. *Tradesmen in the Age of Jefferson.* New York: New York University Press, 1979.

Rodgers, Daniel T. *The Work Ethic in Industrial America, 1850–1920.* Chicago: University of Chicago Press, 1978.

Roe, Joseph Wickham. *English and American Tool Builders.* New Haven: Yale University Press, 1916.

Rosenberg, Nathan. "Anglo-American Wage Differentials in the 1820s." *Journal of Economic History* 27 (June 1967).

————. "Factors Affecting the Diffusion of Technology." *Explorations in Economic History* 10 (Fall 1972).

————. *Perspectives on Technology.* Cambridge, England: Cambridge University Press, 1976.

————. "Technological Change in the Machine Tool Industry, 1840–1910." *Journal of Economic History* 23 (December 1963).

————. *Technology and American Economic Growth.* New York: Harper & Row, Torchbooks, 1972.

————, ed. *The American System of Manufactures: The Report of the Committee on the Machinery of the United States 1855, and the Special Reports of George Wallis and Joseph Whitworth 1854.* Edinburgh: Edinburgh University Press, 1969.

Rostow, W. W. *How It All Began: Origins of the Modern Economy.* New York: McGraw-Hill, 1975.

Rubin, Julius. *Canal or Railroad? Imitation and Innovation in the Response to the Erie Canal in Philadelphia, Baltimore, and Boston. Transactions of the American Philosophical Society,* vol. 51, pt. 7. Philadelphia: American Philosophical Society, 1961.

————. "Urban Growth and Regional Development." In *The Growth of the Seaport Cities, 1790–1825,* edited by David T. Gilchrist. Charlottesville: University Press of Virginia, for the Eleutherian Mills–Hagley Foundation, 1967.

Sampson, Roy J. "American Accounting Education Textbooks and Public Practice prior to 1900." *Business History Review* 31 (Winter 1960).

Sawyer, John E. "The Social Basis of the American System of Manufacturing." *Journal of Economic History* 14 (December 1954).

Schallenberg, Richard H., and David A. Ault. "Raw Materials Supply and Technological Change in the American Charcoal Iron Industry." *Technology and Culture* 18 (September 1977).

Scharf, J. Thomas, and Thompson Westcott. *History of Philadelphia, 1609–1884.* 3 vols. Philadelphia: L. H. Evarts, 1884.

Schmidt, Hubert G. *Rural Hunterdon: An Agricultural History.* New Brunswick: Rutgers University Press, 1946.

Schmookler, Jacob. *Invention and Economic Growth.* Cambridge: Harvard University Press, 1966.

————. *Patents, Invention and Economic Change: Data and Selected Essays.* Edited by Zvi Griliches and Leonid Hurwicz. Cambridge: Harvard University Press, 1972.

Schneider, Louis, and Charles M. Bonjean, eds. *The Idea of Culture in the Social Sciences.* Cambridge, England: At the University Press, 1973.

Sellers, George Escol. *Early Engineering Reminiscences (1815–40) of George Escol Sellers.* Edited by Eugene S. Ferguson. Washington, D.C.: Smithsonian Institution, 1965.

Shepard, James F., and Gary M. Walton. "Economic Change after the American Revolution: Pre and Post War Comparisons of Maritime Shipping and Trade." *Explorations in Economic History* 13 (October 1976).

Sills, David L., ed. *International Encyclopedia of the Social Sciences.* 17 vols. New York: Macmillan and Free Press, 1968.

Sinclair, Bruce. *Philadelphia's Philosopher Mechanics: A History of the Franklin Institute.* Baltimore: Johns Hopkins University Press, 1974.

Singer, Milton. "Culture." In *International Encyclopedia of the Social Sciences*, edited by David L. Sills. Vol. 3. New York: Macmillan and Free Press, 1968.

Siracusa, Carl. *A Mechanical People: Perceptions of the Industrial Order in Massachusetts, 1815–1860.* Middletown, Conn.: Wesleyan University Press, 1979.

Smelser, Neil. *Social Change in the Industrial Revolution: An Application of Theory to the British Cotton Industry.* Chicago: University of Chicago Press, 1959.

Smith, Billy G. "Death and Life in a Colonial Immigrant City: A Demographic Analysis of Philadelphia." *Journal of Economic History* 37 (December 1977).

Smith, David C. *History of Papermaking in the United States (1691–1969).* New York: Lockwood, 1971.

Smith, Merritt Roe. *Harpers Ferry Armory and the New Technology: The Challenge of Change.* Ithaca: Cornell University Press, 1977.

Smith, Walter Buckingham. *Economic Aspects of the Second Bank of the United States.* Cambridge: Harvard University Press, 1953.

Stapleton, Darwin H. "The Transfer of Technology to the United States in the Nineteenth Century." Ph.D. dissertation, University of Delaware, 1975.

Steffen, Charles G. "The Pre-Industrial Iron Worker: Northampton Iron Works, 1780–1820." *Labor History* 20 (Winter 1979).

Stevens, John. *Documents Tending To Prove the Superior Advantages of Railways and Steam Carriages over Canal Navigation.* Reprint. Preface by Arthur H. Cole. Boston: Harvard Business School and the Locomotive Historical Society, 1936.

Storer, J. D. *A Simple History of the Steam Engine.* London: John Baker, 1969.

Stradley, Leighton P. *Early Financial and Economic History of Pennsylvania.* New York: Commerce Clearing House, 1942.

Strassmann, W. Paul. *Risk and Technological Innovation: American Manufacturing Methods during the Nineteenth Century.* Ithaca: Cornell University Press, 1959.

Strickland, William. *Reports on Canals, Railways, Roads and Other Subjects,* Philadelphia: Carey and Lee, 1826.

Sullivan, William A. *The Industrial Worker in Pennsylvania, 1800–1840.* Harrisburg: Pennsylvania Historical and Museum Commission, 1955.

Swank, James M. *History of the Manufacture of Iron in All Ages: And Particularly in the United States for Three Hundred Years, From 1585 to 1885.* Philadelphia: The Author, 1884.

———. *Progressive Pennsylvania: A Record of the Remarkable Industrial Development of the Keystone State.* Philadelphia: Lippincott, 1908.

Sylla, Richard. "American Banking and Growth in the Nineteenth Century: A Partial View of the Terrain." *Explorations in Entrepreneurial History* 2d ser., 9 (Winter 1971–72).

Taussig, F. W. *The Tariff History of the United States.* New York: Putnam's 1899.

Taylor, George R. *The Transportation Revolution, 1815–1860.* New York: Holt, Reinhart, Winston, 1962.

Temin, Peter. *Causal Factors in American Economic Growth in the Nineteenth Century*. London: Macmillan, 1975.

————. *Iron and Steel in Nineteenth-Century America: An Economic Inquiry*. Cambridge: MIT Press, 1964.

————. *The Jacksonian Economy*. New York: Norton, 1969.

————. "Steam and Waterpower in the Early Nineteenth Century." *Journal of Economic History* 26 (June 1976).

————, ed. *The New Economic History*. New York: Penguin, 1973.

Thomas, Robert B. "A Study of the Industry in the Falls of the Schuylkill-Manayunk Area from the Colonia Era to the Civil War." Master's thesis, Temple University, 1960.

Tooker, Elva. *Nathan Trotter, Philadelphia Merchant, 1787–1853*. Cambridge: Harvard University Press, 1955.

Trescott, Paul R. *Financing American Enterprise: The Story of Commercial Banking*. New York: Harper & Row, 1963.

Tryon, Rolla Milton. *Household Manufactures in the United States, 1640–1860: A Study in Industrial History*. Chicago: University of Chicago Press, 1917.

Turnbull, Archibald Douglas. *John Stevens: An American Record*. New York: Century, 1928.

Tyler, David B. *The American Clyde: A History of Iron and Steel Shipbuilding on the Delaware from 1840 to World War I*. Newark, Del.: University of Delaware Press, 1958.

Uselding, Paul. "Conjectural Estimates of Gross Human Capital Inflows to the American Economy." *Explorations in Entrepreneurial History* 2d ser., 9 (Fall 1971).

————. "Studies of Technology in Economic History." In *Recent Developments in the Study of Business and Economic History: Essays in Memory of Herman E. Krooss*, edited by Robert E. Gallman. Greenwich, Conn.: JAI Press, 1977.

————. "Technical Progress at the Springfield Armory, 1820–1850." *Explorations in Economic History*, 2d ser., 9 (Spring 1972).

————, ed. *Business and Economic History: Papers Presented at the Twenty-Fourth Annual Meeting of the Business History Conference*. 2d ser., vol. 7. Urbana: Bureau of Economic and Business Research, 1979.

————, ed. *Research in Economic History*. Greenwich, Conn.: JAI Press, annual, 1976–.

Walker, Joseph E. *Hopewell Village: A Social and Economic History of an Iron-making Community*. Philadelphia: University of Pennsylvania Press, 1966.

Wallace, Anthony F. C. *Culture and Personality*. New York: Random House, 1962.

————. *Rockdale: The Growth of an American Village in the Early Industrial Revolution*. New York: Knopf, 1978.

Walton, Gary M., and James F. Shepard. *The Economic Rise of Early America*. Cambridge, England: Cambridge University Press, 1979.

Wansey, Henry. *Henry Wansey and His American Journal, 1794*. Edited by David John Jeremy. Philadelphia: American Philosophical Society, 1970.

Ware, Caroline F. *The Early New England Cotton Manufacture: A Study of Industrial Beginnings.* Boston: Houghton Mifflin, 1931.

Warner, Sam B. *The Private City: Philadelphia in Three Periods of Its Growth.* Philadelphia: University of Pennsylvania Press, 1968.

Warren, Charles. *Bankruptcy in United States History.* Cambridge, Mass.: Harvard University Press, 1935.

Welsh, Peter C. "Tanning." Hagley Museum Research Report. Greenville, Del.: Eleutherian Mills Historical Library, 1957.

West, E. G. "Literacy and the Industrial Revolution." *Economic History Review* 2d ser., 31 (August 1978).

Wilkinson, Norman B. "Brandywine Borrowings from European Technology." *Technology and Culture* 4 (Winter 1963).

Williamson, Jeffrey G. *American Economic Growth and the Balance of Payments, 1820–1913: A Study of Long Swings.* Chapel Hill: University of North Carolina Press, 1964.

———. "American Prices and Urban Inequality since 1820." *Journal of Economic History* 36 (June 1976).

———. "International Trade and United States Economic Development, 1827–1843." *Journal of Economic History* 21 (September 1961).

———. "The Relative Rental Price of Men, Skills and Machines, 1816–1948." *Journal of Economic History* 27 (June 1967).

Wilson, Thomas. *Picture of Philadelphia for 1824, "Containing the Picture of Philadelphia for 1811 by James Mease, M.D."* Philadelphia: T. Town, 1823.

Wittlinger, Carlton O. "Early Manufacturing in Lancaster County, 1710–1840." *Journal of the Lancaster County Historical Society* 61 (July 1957).

Wolf, Stephanie Grauman. *An Urban Village: Population, Community and Family Structures in Germantown, Pennsylvania.* Princeton: Princeton University Press, 1976.

Woodbury, Robert S. "The Legend of Eli Whitney and Interchangeable Parts." *Technology and Culture* 1 (Summer 1960).

Woodman, Harold D. *King Cotton and His Retainers: Financing and Marketing the Cotton Crop of the South, 1800–1925.* Lexington: University of Kentucky Press, 1968.

Yearley, C. K., Jr. *Enterprise and Anthracite: Economics and Democracy in Schuylkill County, 1820–1875.* Baltimore: Johns Hopkins University Press, 1961.

Zevin, Robert Brooke. *The Growth of Manufacturing in Early Nineteenth-Century New England.* New York: Arno, 1975.

Index